PRAISE FOR *DREAM CATCHERS*

"POPS the Club has provided a critical space for young people affected directly by mass incarceration to voice their hurts, their emptiness, their awareness, and their poetic expressions. I'm awed by the unity of thought, feelings, and words that this writing forges against the odds. Such writing is initiatory, engaging the mythic imagination inherent in us all and birthing the new and unique the way all community-based initiations should do. These anthologies can be examples of the transformation possible in all wounds, making them wombs of new life, energy, and dreams instead of tombs of the dead things we tend to carry when we don't let them go. I honor the work of Amy Friedman and everyone at POPS."

—Luis J. Rodriguez, poet, novelist, journalist, and 2014 Los Angeles Poet Laureate; author of contemporary Chicano literature, notably *Always Running*; winner of the Carl Sandburg Literary Award; and cofounder of Tía Chucha Press

"My father was in prison throughout my teens and I so often felt alone. I cannot imagine how different the experience might have been if I'd had a community like that offered by POPS the Club. I wish I could take *Dream Catchers* and deliver it to my younger self, and with it all the solace, triumph, wisdom, and truth found in its pages. But I need it now too. These are the voices of the more than two million young people in this country with incarcerated parents—full of heartache, hope, insight, and compassion, and we all should listen."

—Tyler Wetherall, author of *No Way Home*

W9-BSY-258

"Nothing on earth tugs on my heartstrings more than kids being hurt, and I know how critical it is to listen to the kids who know all about injustice. The POPS the Club's writers and artists represented in the POPS anthologies have much to teach anyone who is interested in social justice. Their stories, poetry, and artwork overflow with the experiences, wisdom, and insights of those whose lives have been touched by incarceration. They are not to be missed!"

—Scott Budnick, founder of the Anti-Recidivism Coalition and One Community Films and producer of *Just Mercy*

"Parental and familial incarceration has destabilized families and communities throughout the United States. Our children, this country's most precious commodity, have been affected more than any group. Many of them suffer in silence, unable to articulate their pain, their suffering, and oftentimes their shame. This collection of brilliance has provided those directly impacted with a mechanism to amplify their voices so that their stories can be heard and understood. This work will educate, positively influence, and empower every reader. It serves as a testament to the resilience, power, and intelligence of every single contributor. We all should be grateful for what these beautiful souls have created for our benefit."

—Tony Lewis Jr., activist and author of *Slugg*

"As a woman who grew up with an incarcerated parent, I know how challenging being a teenager with a loved one in prison can be. POPS the Club gives high schoolers a voice, offering them opportunities to talk about it, write about it, and feel part of an ever-growing community. This collection of memories, thoughts, and ambitions represents the toll that everyone touched by the system knows. Through their pages, the writers and artists have found a rare form of empowerment."

—Deanna M. Paul, journalist

"The diverse and powerful voices in *Dream Catchers* bear witness to the pain, heartache, and triumphs of everyday high schoolers touched by incarceration. In an age where the news is rife with stories of family separation and children being locked in cages, these poems, stories, and drawings have never been more relevant—or urgent."

—Laurie Sandell, author of *The Impostor's Daughter* and *Truth and Consequences*

"*Dream Catchers* is a must-read for directly impacted individuals and their allies. By bringing the voices of the youth to the forefront, POPS the Club gives readers unprecedented access to the experience of familial incarceration by the experts themselves—directly impacted individuals."

—Whitney Hollins, PhD, educator, advocate, and author of *Anna's Test*

"For twenty years I've transformed concepts to creations, helping dozens of authors find success in the marketplace, many becoming *New York Times* bestselling authors. I know what it takes to develop a compelling message, and I know powerful books and important messages when I read them. The POPS the Club anthologies are monumental works of vital, inspiring stories we all need to read."

—Kristin Loberg, collaborator on *Grain Brain, Hype,* and *The Switch*

"I can't think of a better way to convey the heartbreak and hardships of having an incarcerated family member than the POPS anthologies. I've seen many people (including myself) brought to tears by the gorgeous, honest poetry, essays, and artwork in *Dream Catchers*. It shines a brilliant light into a part of our country that too often is left in shadow."

—Claire LaZebnik, author of *Epic Fail, Things I Should Have Known,* and *The Smart One and the Pretty One* and coauthor with Dr. Lynn Koegel of *Overcoming Autism*

"What is most impressive about the POPS anthologies is the overwhelming power of the truth and sincerity contained within their pages. In *Dream Catchers*, each story is heartfelt, honest, open, and fearless. The teenaged authors have voluntarily bared their souls in order that they might lighten their own psychic burden and maybe, just maybe, invent a better life for themselves. Short stories, poems, song lyrics, and artworks will last as long as these books exist, and the young contributors have made themselves immortal. Such an impressive accomplishment, and something that should be supported by reading *Dream Catchers* and all the POPS anthologies."

—Damien Belliveau, motion picture editor, author, and creator
   of *The PartBlack Project*

"Through writing and art, discussion and community, POPS heals the stigma and shame so often felt by youth whose lives have been impacted by prison. They are the silent victims of our mass incarceration crisis. POPS should be in every high school in America, and its books, like *Dream Catchers*, should be in every classroom."

—Christina McDowell, author of *After Perfect* and *The Cave Dwellers* and coproducer of *A Survivor's Guide to Prison*

"*Dream Catchers* is a masterpiece of light-handed art: stories and perspectives from the children who pay the price of a growing carceral state. Reading this work forces us to see the human deficit of torn families and spirals of harm that our worship of nonrestorative procedural justice propagates. Above all, the bittersweet richness comes from the hope and resilience present on the page. Without shame, the young writers in these pages use their skill and clarity to find both solace for themselves and salvation for all of us."

—Robert Pollock, teaching artist and manager of the Prison
   and Justice Writing Program, PEN America, and illustrator of
   Sing, Sing, Midnight

"*Dream Catchers* is a unique experience—a collection of poems, essays, and artwork that intimately connect us to a population of teenagers who are navigating life in a very particular way. These teens share their work with brave authenticity and a maturity well beyond their years. The work is powerful, heartbreaking, inspiring, and sobering. A must-read for anyone who truly cares to know the full impact of our prison system."

—Jessica Tuck, actor, producer, and founder and executive producer of Spark Off Rose

"During the 1980s and '90s, one of my most talented creative writing students lived in constant fear that her father would be sent back to jail merely for walking down a block where drugs were being sold. She and many other students lived with the shame that someone they loved had been incarcerated. Had POPS existed in those days, my students wouldn't have had to feel so afraid or ashamed, because they would have been in a community of people who could sympathize with them and give them practical advice. And they might have fought despair by helping others with similar problems and by expressing their own feelings in poems and stories that would make them proud. Everyone will be inspired by the powerful work in *Dream Catchers*."

—Stephen O'Connor, author of *Will My Name Be Shouted Out?*

"I found myself awestruck by these writers and artists impacted by mass incarceration. Their power to observe and to transform not only stigma around incarcerated people but their own pain, shame, and longing into something beautiful and lasting is worthy of much praise and thanks. I'm grateful they trusted us with this work, that we can step into their lives, however briefly."

—Michelle Franke, Executive Director, PEN America Los Angeles

"The first public reading by writers of the POPS anthologies back in 2015, presented at the Grove Barnes and Noble in Los Angeles, was a memorable and emotional event. Witnessing these new writers, nurtured by the POPS program, as they felt the power of their words, their stories—spoken in public and appearing physically in print—was a thrilling reminder of the roots of what we do as writers and why. I have no doubt that I heard voices for the first time that day that we will be hearing from in the future, and *Dream Catchers* is evidence of that!"

—Thomas Frick, art critic, museum editor, and author of *The Iron Boys*

"In *Dream Catchers*, young people bear witness to the pain, hardship, and multigenerational repercussions inflicted by our flawed prison system. With their poems, memoirs, and stories—beautiful, authentic, angry, yearning—we grasp in a profound way the human toll our mass incarceration policies exact on children and their families. As these works give voice to the youths who wrote them, they also empower us to deeper self-scrutiny and political action."

—Deborah A. Lott, author of *Don't Go Crazy without Me* and instructor of creative writing and literature, Antioch University, Los Angeles

Dream Catchers

POPS the Club Anthology

Out of the Woods Press

Out of the Woods Press
www.outofthewoodspress.com

Quantity sales. Special discounts are available on quantity purchases by corporations, associations, and others. For details, contact the "Special Sales Department" at the address above.

Orders by US trade bookstores and wholesalers. Please contact BCH: (800) 431-1579 or visit www.bookch.com for details.

Printed in the United States of America

Cataloging-in-Publication Data

Names: POPS the Club, author. | Friedman, Amy, editor. | Danziger, Dennis, 1951-, editor.
Title: Dream catchers : POPS the Club anthology / [edited by Amy Friedman and Dennis Danziger.]
Description: Los Angeles, CA: Out of the Woods Press, 2020.
Identifiers: LCCN: 2020909607 | ISBN 978-1-952197-06-2
Subjects: High school students' writings, American. | Teenagers' writings. | High school students--Literary collections. | BISAC LITERARY COLLECTIONS / General | YOUNG ADULT NONFICTION / Family / General
Classification: LCC PS508.S43 P06 2020 | DDC 810.8--dc23

First Edition
25 24 23 22 21   10 9 8 7 6 5 4 3 2 1

Cover designer: TLC Graphics
Editors: Amy Friedman and Dennis Danziger
Interior designer: Marin Bookworks

In a room where
people unanimously maintain
a conspiracy of silence,
one word of truth
sounds like a pistol shot.

– *Czeslaw Milosz*

"POPS," Janna Rae Nieto

Contents

Where We Grow From

No Bars

When We Were Kids

Disorder in the House

The Real and the Imagined

Roads to Freedom

Keep Us in Your Heart

Almost Adults

Introduction
Perspectives of a POPS Club Advisor

Dear Pops the Club students,

We absolutely *hate* that you are here. We loathe it, actually. We detest that anyone as awesome as you ever has to walk through our doors carrying the burden of "tough stuff." It's not fair. You know it and we know it. We both wish things could be different. We want to come into your lives armed with a magic eraser and get rid of all the mess you have to deal with. We don't want to have to run a club for students affected by incarceration. We like art and flower-arranging clubs—heck, even clubs about motorcycles and sports are better than clubs about prison, right?

But in the same breath, we *love* that you are here. Your smiles, your participation, and your resilience astound us. We love that you come to us vulnerable yet not afraid to share your deepest and darkest dirt. What you don't realize is that when you share your challenges, you give others the opportunity to let some of their own challenges go. You have so much strength in your own stories, and you don't even know it. You are spreading hope to each and every one of us. We learn from you every day. Your presence in POPS has created a family within our school walls that is precious and important. We love that we have an opportunity to be your advisor and, most important, your friend.

We want you to know that we admire you. We think that these experiences you have been a part of are going to mold you into adults who are compassionate and aware of others' feelings and circumstances. We know that you have taken hold of your pain and turned it into positive energy, and that you are going to put it out into the world for others to benefit from. We see you all growing in amazing ways. Your stories touch us. Sometimes we cry with you, and sometimes we wait till we get home to cry your tears. We laugh with you because you bring us joy among the sorrow we share. Sometimes we don't always know the right things to say, but we always listen. We always leave our meetings hopeful for your future, because you have no bigger cheerleader than us.

We want you to know something else. We struggle too. Please don't think that because you are a teenager with these circumstances in your life that you are the only ones. Adults have problems too. We share the same dreams, goals, sorrows, and challenges. We are all walking down the same road, and we are thankful that we get to join you in this journey.

We want to thank you POPS club students for everything you have given to us. Every week we prepare a meal to share with you, and in return you fill our hearts with connection and purpose. I can't think of a better club to be a member of.

We *hate* that we *love* POPS as much as we do—but it's true. Thank you for sharing your lives with us. Never stop speaking up, speaking out, and telling your truth. Never be ashamed to share that prison is part of your story. It's part of our story too.

We *love* you,

Jennifer Morrison and your proud POPS club advisors

"*Dance,*" *Janna Rae Nieto*

Day In, Day Out

Who I Am

Imari Stevenson

Stressed and depressed
But I ALWAYS
keep a smile on my face
so that they only see me when I'm at my best.

"Band-Aids Don't Fix Everything," Reagan King

Never Give Up

Ahidsa Mateo

Never give up
Because you're telling yourself that you are worthless
Keep trying harder

Never give up
Because you're setting yourself up for failure
Give it your best shot

Never give up
Because you're making a big mistake
Believe in yourself, never fear

Never give up
Don't let your dreams down
Whatever you started, finish it

"People," Janna Rea Nieto

Scribbled Thoughts

Jazmin Joseph

Stop acting like you don't care
I'm ignoring the past ignores
Scribbled thoughts in my head
But don't even bother to color them in
See, look, I was doing just fine
Until you came up
And wasted my time
Trying to figure out what I did wrong
It all made no sense
Listening to my friends
Knowing I'm hardheaded
I stay wrapped in my head
And they wonder why I'm on mute
Quit acting like you got no clue
So I can let loose

Mind, Body, and Paint

John Rodriguez

I'm relaxing my mind, sitting on my bed, letting the music massage my ears. I'm looking out the window, watching the sun's every move, waiting for it to set. The whole time I'm in my room writing, killing time waiting for my parents to fall asleep. I'm practicing different styles, making sure to get them stuck in my head. I peek out my bedroom door. It looks as if the coast is clear. I slide my closet door open, slip on my black Levis, a black t-shirt, and the dirtiest black shoes I can find. I open up the top drawer of my dresser and gather my tips. I pick out the finest colors of paint. I unzip my backpack and stuff all my needs toward the bottom. Now I'm off.

I slowly open my front door. I hold my breath and take light steps. Now I'm outside. The cold air hits my face and wakes me right up. It has me eager to get there. I walk through this mellow city, Inglewood, California. The streets are quiet. Walking down each block, I can hear my every footstep. The cans in my backpack rattle. I glance left, right. All I see are light poles and parked cars. No people. I'm near. I look around to see if there are any cops or people who might call the cops while I'm jumping in.

"Lights," Alba Navas

I'm in! My feet hit the dirt. It smells as if I landed in a nursery. The floor is covered with branches. The gigantic gray walls that surround me are covered with tagging. My heart is pounding. I look to the heavens and all I see are the blurred clouds. I make my way down the hill. The branches are constantly causing me to lose my balance. I take every step carefully. I'm at the bottom of the hill. I glance toward my right. Cars speeding at 70, 80 mph. I take a deep breath. I make my run for it across the 405 Freeway. The headlights coming my way are blinding me. My ears are crying from the cars' obnoxious honking.

Thank God I make it across the freeway safely. I'm now near the exit on Manchester Boulevard. I can see the wall staring at me. It's the wall I've been wanting to hit. It's beautiful. I love the way the wall is positioned so that when people are driving by, it clearly stands out.

"Art of the Ghetto," Julian Izaguirre

I approach the wall. I take a breather and rip my backpack open. I pull out my spray cans. My hand immediately bonds with it. I feel the coldness of its skin. I can hear it screaming my name. I put my "New York Fat" tip on the can because in my eyes it's perfect. The way the tip flares the paint out and the thickness of the lines is just right, not too wide, not too skinny.

I'm spraying away, letting my hand guide itself, letting it go free. The paint comes out, getting a right grip on the wall, leaving a trace of fine lines. I'm rotating the can as I write, getting the perfect flare and thickness of the line. While I'm writing, my body purifies itself—relieving itself of my stress and helping me forget my worries. No more getting screamed at by my mother. No one is telling me what to do. There is no better feeling than this. I'm in another world. Nothing bothers me. It's just me, the wall, and the can, doing what I do best.

This is my home.

Sleepless Nights

Jazmin Joseph

My thoughts pile up,
My heart speeds up,
My body heats up,
My covers tighten up,
I am stuck.
I am lost inside my thoughts, thinking the worst.
I do not know why I overthink so much.
I question so much that I scare myself.
Is it because I don't want to come up with an answer?
Or am I preparing myself?
But what would I be preparing myself for?
There I go again.
I snap myself out of those wild thoughts.
My heart slows down,
My body cools down,
My covers loosen up,
And I am free.

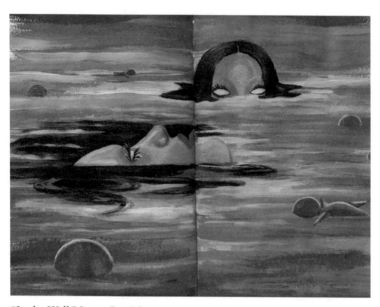

"In the Well," Janna Rae Nieto

My Kind

P.J. Swanson

Recently, I've been pretending a lot, faking, lying, not necessarily to others, mostly to myself.

I have been trying to think of ways to try and conform to the rules of "society" and such. Growing up, it had always been pretty straightforward, and I always knew what to expect. Maybe that was because I had an older sibling to guide me through it, or maybe it was because I was made to believe that I always had a net beneath me, a safety net, one that was tight and would never let me fall. Said net was made up of many people I was taught to trust and rely upon. But nothing is indestructible.

Nets rip. Life goes on. Years go by, time tends to fly, but my head will never end, the spinning will never come to a halt. And forever in the back of my mind there sits a tiny bubble, a bubble of thoughts, if you will. . . . Sometimes this bubble resurfaces, sometimes it just sits there in the shadows, waiting in the dark for the perfect moment to pounce.

There is no going away. There are ways of lessening it. But both parties seem to just try and "leave well enough alone." Little do they know that "well enough" still causes pain, still tears apart, still confuses and shocks. That bubble will never be popped.

I don't need you here with me. I am not requesting for you to respond or even fully acknowledge me. I don't want redemption. I don't want a name or place in your life. I just want the time of day, just a moment for you to take a breath, breathe, and maybe, just maybe, you can put in the effort to recognize my kind.

I Am

Victor Zapata

I'm a liar
I'm a cheater
Don't trust me
I'm selfish
And I'll deceive you.

I'll take the knife behind my back and stick it in yours
And I'll laugh until I can't breathe anymore
Then ask if you're okay
and stick the knife in some more
I'll deceive you.

And if you need me I won't be there
I'm at home watching a movie
You can call and ask for help
I'll look at my phone until it stops ringing
And in the morning I'll say, "Sorry, I was sleeping."
I'm a liar.

I have no money
I'm broke
I just paid rent and my phone bill
But on Snapchat I'm out at the club posting my drinks
    and taking shots with the people I'm with
I'm selfish.

I don't love you
I said it because you said it
I lock my phone and delete my texts

Sometimes I text you good night
And go out with some people I never met
I'm a cheater.

I'm a liar
I'm a cheater
Don't trust me
I'm selfish
And I'll deceive you.

The Paint

Julian Izaguirre

What am I to you, another news article? Or am I a statistic? Are you calculating my grades to see if I qualify for prison? Or do you want to give me a fair chance and qualify me for food stamps?

I don't know that struggle of surviving off of stamps, but I know what it's like to be called that bean who sits in the back. Tell me, why is it that growing up without a father is the norm for a lot of us? 'Cause we all grow up to be equal in some way. Why is it that we can't have what other people have? Why do the minorities have to be the ones to stay sad? Why can't we strive like they do without straying from our cultures? Why do we gotta apply to this world built for the white ones? Why is it that I need the stellar grades and a test made for the college kids to get accepted to a school of art? Why do I have to be the one to bust my ass to end up living like the next guy when the next guy looks me in the eye and says I've had this since I was knee high? Why do I have to struggle with family in 'n out just for them to feel like they're helping us out by slangin' rocks? Why do I have to sit here and tell you my life story? Because my life story is the one that helps me build to what I want to be.

Here's the breakdown: I grew up with a broken father going in 'n out. I had a brother who constantly got stereotyped and with cousins who followed the role model. To them the streets were all they needed, because that's all they saw. With them in prison it was just me, my bro, and my momma who I've got all the love in the world for.

You want the paint? Take this for the paint. You look at me and see broken, and you see a kid who's hopeless, but if you were in my shoes you'd know that hopeless leads to homeless and homeless is what I've seen growing up 'cause my aunt is there now, yet it all boils down to me.

Take the canvas: an apartment filled to the brim with people sleeping on the floors, people showering in the wee hours of the morning just to make it to school on time. A block being gentrified to run our people out of it so the other ones can live there while we're all on the run.

What? You still want more? I'll help you like Bob Ross once told me, and I'll apply the liquid white. A kid going to school with hopes being crushed by people telling him he wasn't shit, but he keeps his hopes high so he can make it out of that ditch.

Then you want me to tell you where everyone is? Lemme break it down again. My cousins are living happy lives, same goes for me and my brother. Living happily with a nephew who brings me joy, with a grandmother whose face lights up every time she sees us, and a mom who gets happy every time she hears us. My aunt, may God have mercy on her soul, who I pray for every day to wake up and hear the birds chirping. . . .

There's your paint, sir. I gave you all the tools and you want me to tell you more? Use what I gave you and do me a favor . . . paint the f'ing picture.

"Portrait of Julian," Chris Wright

Know This

I AM ME

Hello, I'm a sophmore at Culver City high school. I am a member of POPS club and enjoy learning about the guest speakers' experiences. I also love how welcome and comfortable I feel when I walk in the room. I love to bake, read, and listen to music. I also like to write because it helps me release my emotions. Whenever there is a bumpy road in life, I always try to keep a positive mindset by telling myself that it'll all be worth it at the end. So that's why I never give up and keep going through the bumpy road.

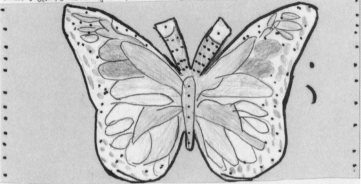

Not everyday is perfect, sometimes I feel angry, alone, different, sad, anxious, happy, embrassed, but every emotion serves a purpose, that's just apart of life. The dark gloomy days ultimately lead to sunny spring days. before you succeed you have to fail numerous times, there's always going to be light at the end, does not matter how dim the light is, there still some type of glow. Never give up! I am ME

MIXED Emotions;

Mixed Emotions/

"*Mixed Emotions*," Morgan Hamilton

What I Want My Parents to Know...
but Don't Want to Tell Them

Members of the Venice High School POPS club

I had sex. I smoke. I used to be suicidal. I've cut myself. I still get depressed sometimes. I almost killed myself.

I don't like being around my dad. I can't look him in the eye without feeling awkward. I feel like I don't know who he is because he's been gone for so long. He frustrates me. I don't want him in my life sometimes.

I want my parents to know that I feel so alone. I look for comfort in others who I know don't care about me. I want my parents to know that their words hurt. I want my parents to know I have no idea what I'm doing with myself.

Dad, I want you to know that every day I feel like I disappoint you. I try so hard to try and make up for it, but I still feel like I'm not good enough. But I will never tell you this because I'm afraid I might actually be a disappointment.

Mom, I want to ask more about my father but I'm scared of your response. Mom, I don't want you to see my grades. Just because I don't talk about school doesn't mean I don't care about my education.

Mom, I want you to know that I might be bisexual because I kind of like girls. I know I'm not supposed to but I can't help what I like.

"Wonderland," Janna Rae Nieto

I want my mom to know her snide, judgmental comments and negative attitude make me hate living with her. I'm embarrassed to go out in public with her because she always has something to say to or about someone. Love you, tho.

I can't go back to New York (65th & Ingleside). I used to serve crack. And can't forget the memories.

I want my parents to know I love them. I want them to know why I am the way I am. I want them to know my reasons. I want them to know not everything is easy.

I want them to know but I can't tell them that I'm gay and have a partner.

I want my parents to know that every day I feel more and more distance between us. I feel that I won't want to return home when I leave next year because what is there to return to?

What I want my mom to know but can't tell her is:

> When you are having a bad day, it rubs off on the household.
> You start yelling at us about the house not being clean, but you live here too.
> Therefore, that makes you at fault as well.
> Stop blaming us for everything.
> Put the blame on yourself for lashing out at us when we didn't do anything to you.
> We are tired of the nonsense.

"Six-Word Memoir," Erika Hernandez

Advice to Ninth-Graders

John Bembry

Embrace every change and decide wisely.

Don't fall for peer pressure. Love yourself and your health.

Teachers don't pick on students for no reason, they want you to use your abilities to the fullest.

Find what you love to do if you haven't already.

Stay true to what you believe.

Everything is not about popularity, it's about your future.

Let love find you and you will love it.

Party hard, you will be working hard very soon.

Don't be afraid to let your genuine friends know you love them and appreciate the memories.

Don't procrastinate about your grades.

As a senior I was on probation, attending 8 periods and doing an adult school program for the credits I needed to walk the stage.

I barely made it.

Not only that, I was able to speak my heart-written experience to all my peers before leaving Venice High.

Make your mark on the world.

Leave behind something more than a memory.

Ronald's 5 Rules for Freshmen

Ronald Griffis

You don't have to like your teachers, but when they give advice, take it.

Avoid being a follower.

Be your own self.

Stay away from drugs.

Whenever you need help, ask for it.

Advice

Anonymous

Not everyone's opinion matters.

Be happy.

More Wisdom

Talena Vasquez

Being late a few times will not ruin your life.

Don't let a bad five minutes affect your whole 24 hours.

"Palos Verdes Moon," Reggie Love Hurd

Handshakes

Guillermo Ovalle

No particular meaning for each one
Each one is built by
Any number of individuals
To represent
A promise
A friendship
A relationship
So much can be said
From the way it's created
To the way it's executed

Some make handshakes to impress others
Some use them to feel secure
But they are all backed up by the same motive
Appreciation for someone else

I personally like
the specialty of a handshake
As well as the other person
There's no better sign
to signify a friendship
Than something that's special between
Friends or soulmates

From friendship bracelets
To matching tattoos
The connection stays there
Even if things go south
Once your own version

of a handshake
Is shown its true colors
Everything turns out fine
you feel safe
Secure
Protected

Where We Grow From

"Self-Love," Reagan King

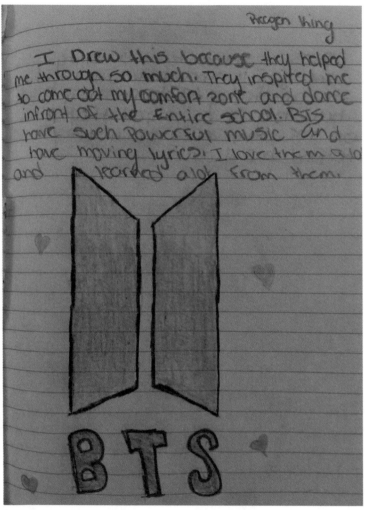

Reagan King

I Drew this because they helped me through so much. They inspired me to come out my comfort zone and dance infront of the Entire school. BTS have such Powerful music and have moving lyrics. I love them a lot and learned a lot from them.

BTS

"My Journal," Reagan King

You Are My Home

Stacie Ramirez

You might have to stay away from me, far from me, far from him, but it was your actions, your words, your decision that made it come down to this.

Now you have a limit of how close you can get to me, talk to me, or see me. You might be the one with the limits, you might feel like the one trapped inside, but you lost, and I lost.

You having to stay away took away my best friend, my favorite good morning and my favorite good night, my favorite hug, my peace, my reason to live, and my happiness. I miss you. I miss your meals, your hugs, your smile, your laugh, your warmth, and our cheesy inside jokes. How could I ever replace you? When you were taken from me, and I was taken from you, what could I do but stay away? You are my home and I have to stay away from you; it seemed so unfair, so unjust. I was upset at you for so long because you put us in this situation, you let it get this far, and to me you were the only one to blame.

But I love you, and I just want to be with you. Our lives will never be the same, and that makes me sad all the time because even if I wished it could be I know what our reality is. I'm hopeful that we can make it work. No matter how distant we are, I know we'll find our way back to each other, and even if you have your flaws, I'll stay to see you grow out of them for us.

Because I need you more than ever. You are my home.

The House

Angela Fajardo

In 2020 yes we move forward
The next task
Yet looking back

Facing the loss

The house is humanly empty
Yet
Full of Spirits
Full of people
I close my eyes and they appear
La Abuelita
El Abuelito
La Tía Matilde
El Tío Chuchu
The faded memory of my *Tío Ernesto*

Their presence lingers
Their strength
Their fortitude
Their arms
Their warmth

Vivir entre los muertos
To live among the ones not physically here
The house

I Come From

Alba Navas

I come from thick fingertips with dirt-filled gaps
I come from walls so thick, you could hear a voice crack
I come from being the outsider no one dared to look at
I come from the aftershocks of honesty
But I grow from aching joints running past the finish line
I grow from glossy, droopy eyes, writing through the night
I grow from hearing "no" too many times
Where I grow from is more than where I come from

Growing Up in the Hood

Katherine Secaida

I come from the hood where the birds are so huge they
   look like helicopters
I come from the hood where on Christmas, cars with red
   and blue lights spark our neighborhood
I come from the hood where they make art with one color
I come from the hood, but that doesn't mean I need to
   look or talk hood
I come from the hood but that doesn't mean I don't own a
   book . . .
I make my own!

I Don't Remember Much

Blue

I don't remember much of my childhood, but a memory strong in me is the orange tree in the front lawn of the z-house I once lived in. No matter the season the oranges were always sour. The front lawn wasn't maintained well, and it was mostly dirt with patches of faded grass. All that stood there was a brittle tree, with fruit that weighed the tree down.

I Come From

Maricela Romero

I come from Venice, California; 6th Street on the west
    side of Lincoln
I come from bullet holes in the walls, the CaCa's tried
    stealing your cousin's life
I come from where "trust" and "love" are words with no
    true meaning
I come from drugs and alcohol being everyone's escape
I come from thanking God for every breath because you
    never know when it's going to be your last
I come from the Ghost Town on the west side of Lincoln
    where we ain't scared to play

I Love my Bed

Celine

I love my bed. My bed lets me rest after a good day. My bed lets my thoughts go wild. My bed puts me to sleep after I've cried, it's the only safe zone I've got. The only place I feel safe, and even if it's not my bed, it's a bed I can sleep in and dream, and dream all night. And dream again and let my thoughts run free as I sleep in my bed.

Anxiety

J/U

Anxious . . .
My bed, a place to hide away.
White, blank, and lifeless, yet so pure.

Clockwise

Elena Bernardez

The sky in Honduras is light and beautiful
It's hot and burning
Melting like an ice cream
You feel you want to cannonball into a cool pool
Jumping off the rock into the cool water
Slipping on the mossy rock was so painful I cried

When the sun rises it's beautiful
Silver gray clouds floating in the back
My fears of the past
Haunting black pain
Nightmare

When I was hurt
The sun healed me as it rose
When I was in pain
When I was torn to pieces
When I am in my room
Hiding in the blanket
I can't breathe
I feel that I am collapsing
I am falling into the dark pit

I am a seed
In the dirt, breaking apart
Shattered heart
Everything in my life is crushed
Death of growth
Not going to kill me

The stem will heal me
Help me rise up and bring me water
Wash me down
Wash all the pain the seed has been through

The joy of seeing my grandfather walking quickly
with his cane
White and blue like the color of the Honduras flag
Happy to see me and my brothers and mom
Then finding out my grandfather has become the
soil again
When petals die
They end up growing back
Rebirth
Like people in my life
The way we laugh and dance
Eating fresh mango from
His tree

I feel my leaves are breaking
Petals are falling down
The sun is giving us a light to grow back
A beautiful tiger lily sprouts from the seed

"Palms," Alba Navas

I Come from Waking Up to my Parents Arguing

Anonymous

I come from waking up to my parents arguing. A family that pretends to be happy, but as soon as that door closes they can't stand each other.

I come from growing up scared to talk to my mom, knowing if I say something that she doesn't like I'll get slapped.

I come from being the youngest of three.

I come from if I don't wear pink dresses or skirts, I'm not a girly girl.

I come from my dad not spending time with me because he is always working.

I come from having an older brother who will beat up any guy I talk to.

I come from walking home at night because my parents are working.

I come from having to choose which parent I want to live with.

I come from choosing which parent I want to spend the rest of my life with.

I come from having to lie to my mom about who I'm with and where I am.

I come from preferring to be at school than at my house.

I come from Culver City.

Haiku

Anonymous

I have nine brothers
All from different mothers
But they are tricksters

"Tricksters," Janna Rae Nieto

Me Nombraron Después de Ella
("They Named Me After Her")

Donaji Garcia

Every family has a voice, a history
Printed with refined *voces del pasado*
Speaking Zapoteco (indigenous language)
And calling me with open arms,
Wrists wrapped around *semanarios*
Whispering, *"Donají, su nombre es Donají."*
Behind my infant ears I could listen to *el cantar del
    río Atoyac*
Where winter once brought a timeless *lirio*
And an unforgettable fragrance of peace toward
    her people.
Donají was a princess who fell in love with Nucano,
    a prince
So beautiful and yet the enemy of her *gente*
Yet she treated his wounds and protected him
Then set him free like the caged bird
To later be decapitated to be found
With a blossomed *flor*
And an everlasting *amor*
Remembered *siglos después una leyenda*
As my name
Pronounced differently through every tongue
But *mi identidad* is still with me
Follows me as I carry my ID card
And the name flows down the river . . .
Repeatedly heard
Orgullosamente Oaxaqueña.

I Come from a Bold City

Hayden Brown

I come from a bold city
I come from a place where if you don't take your chance,
    you won't have another one
I come from a place where there is always someone better
I come from a Babylon of the present world
A city ahead of the entire world
I come from the City of Angels

"Connected Detachment," Nicole Bezerra

"Confusing Journey," Nicole Bezerra

The Mathematics of Life

Eric Lee

Life, in some abstract way, is very mathematical. Like mathematical constants, there are constants in everyone's life. These constants, however, are unlike mathematical constants in that they are an illusion—because the reality of life is nothing is constant. Mountains weather away. Canyons erode into dust. People come and go. Relationships are born and then they die. Everything is ever changing and nothing is constant. Consistency is an illusion.

Today my 15-year-old fish fell ill. He was a constant in my life; always relentlessly swimming around in his tank, facing life with a vigor I've never seen in a creature, especially considering his lack of fins. My fish was a rock, one of the few constants in my life. Now it looks as if he may die. The hazy water of his tank is like the smoky illusion that is consistency. As he withers away, so will the rest of the world, because nothing is constant. It's the universe's way of taunting us, showing how little control we have over our own lives. With every passing second, entropy shall make certain that we are not.

Embroidered on the Cempasuchil Flower

Donaji Garcia

Aztec lovers
Young and affectionate both raised together
Like the fruit and the tree
Xóchitl and Huitzilin
United as the wind carried both of them to the
Top of the mountain
Offering *flores* to Tonatiuh, *el dios del sol,*
Prometiendo el eterno amor
Until a war began
And Huitzilin's death followed
Llanto lleno el ser de su amada
As her legs carried her one last time up the *montaña*
To plead to Tonatiuh to her love to be complete
Y las oraciones fueron escuchadas
As she transformed into a radiant flower
Covered in petals with the colors of the sun
Beautifully *abierta*
With 20 *pétalos* each overlapping another
Cherished days
Un colibrí embraced the flower with its beak
Huitzilin was with her and she was
Part of a forever union
Beyond *la muerte*
Who will never put them apart.
And every Día de Muertos
I recall *su historia*
And I feel like my loved ones
Están junto a mi.

I Come From Asking Too Many Questions

Matthew Lopez

Confusion as a young boy, asking why people would come and go in the family. Watching people with everything that they ever wanted. Taking trips to places at times that seemed as if they were in the middle of nowhere. Then watching everything they had go away.

I come from asking too many questions to being quiet and observant. Seeing family argue and leave, to coming back with forgiveness.

I come from worrying about hearing banging on the door at 2 or 3 in the morning, to it making sense piece by piece.

I come from being confused to being a puzzle solver and putting it all together.

In the end, it all made sense.

"Abstract," Richard Anthony Espinoza

Family Can Hate You Too

Giselle Sanchez

1. I will tear the old man apart, his skin, his bones, all will decompose, and his hate will set his obnoxious soul aflame.

2. This compulsive hatred that he seems to hold inside will spread faster than the speed of light.

3. Initiating a fiery rage that should have been extinguished at its first spark.

4. I know he'll ask himself . . . Who will come to my rescue?

5. Who will come and try to bring peace to my soul?

6. Who will come to put out this angry fire inside me?

7. He better not think of me because I swear . . . this time it won't be me.

8. Can't he see?

9. It's too late for that, but he'll go on and speak out of hate. He'll tell me how good I am at loving others when I struggle to love and accept my own fate.

10. He'll go on and spill the tea with the rest of our family.

11. He'll tell them all about my insecurities, how he seems to believe he has preposterous power over me.

12. The power to slither his way into my thoughts and contaminate my aura at night.

13. He's a dangerous snake. Bastard will go on and spit his venomous words right at my face.

14. I know his kind, always malicious and stupidly ambitious. It is nothing new.

15. His words are bullets, and his mouth's the gun; I know he'll pull the trigger, and might leave my body too brittle.

16. But I have spent many years building a wall, strong as the woman who gave me my life.

"Nobody's Goddess," Janna Rae Nieto

Spanglish

Donaji Garcia

A foreign language was my first song.
I was blossoming in between our
Rancheras and *jarabes*
Shoving tamales and speaking a different tongue.
Rolling my r's through the river of my ancestry,
Crossing the rocks.
I walked on the concrete floor with huaraches and the sunny
Skies poured its perfume on my indigenous skin.
I am defined as a Latina, a Mexican-American, a Chicana.
We pray to La Virgen with painted *rosas* on our *trenzas*
And worker hands we devote to
The 21st Century . . .
The 5th Sun of the Aztecs . . .
Mestizos reigning in the town that was once Tenochtitlan . . .
We adopted English . . .
Yet we threw our identity away . . .
Or we mixed it into a salad . . .
With its own dressing of *acentos* . . .
Mezclado en la sociedad . . .
Disappearing what was once made . . .
Would just be seen as if through tears on the screen.

No Bars

"Dream," Janna Rae Nieto

POPS

Leslie Mateos

I wrote this for a presentation for middle-school children of the incarcerated who participated in The Share & Care Program, where I was invited to talk to them about my life experiences and my experience with POPS the Club when I was in high school.

I joined POPS when I was a senior in high school.

Many people see us and think we're okay, having a beautiful life, not having to worry about anything. What they don't see is the struggle we are going through. They just see the mask we wear every day.

And that's how I felt for years, until I joined POPS. I felt so ashamed of who I was, of where I came from. I was ashamed of people knowing that my dad was deported when I was 7. I was ashamed of being the daughter of a prisoner, the daughter of an alcoholic, granddaughter of an alcoholic, having cousins who spent time in and out of cells.

It's horrible living afraid that one day one of them isn't going to come home. Keeping all of that inside of you is hard.

When I was in middle school, I always acted strong, pretending everything was all right, but there were days when the depression would overtake me. I'd lock myself in the bathroom, turn on the shower, put on some loud music and cry it all out, and then walk out as if nothing had happened.

That's the strategy I had before joining POPS.

Joining POPS helped me understand that I wasn't the only one going through a situation like that. I wasn't the only one with a family member in prison. I was so surprised when I saw many people I already knew in the room.

There's a saying that appearances can be deceiving. And it's true. You can see a person looking happy when in reality they're dying on the inside. I always tried to be the type of girl who'd be there for people when they needed a friend.

I'm here to tell you guys that you are not alone. There's no reason to be ashamed.

We have to hold our heads up high and show the world we can be somebody new.

When I Was Four Years Old

Xavier Tucker

When I was four years old my uncle had some trouble trying to stay out of jail. He ran from the police a lot. One night he told me he would be right back, but when I woke up he wasn't back.

My uncle went to jail till he was 45. He was in jail for 20 years, and I was very upset. I don't want to go to jail. I have heard a lot about jail, and some things are inappropriate.

To not go to jail I will change my ways and get my life together.

"Freedom," Janna Rae Nieto

Jail Is Not the Place to Be

Xavious Anderson

I'm going to tell you why jail is not the place to be, and how to stay out of trouble.

Jail is not the right place because when in the "land fill" you're never safe, and you could always be or feel uncomfortable. You could be uncomfortable by inmates intimidating you, by guards or inmates making aggressive moves, which could result in injury or death. Also, the worst thing about jail is Death Row, because you're taking your last meals and breaths.

In life, you can stay out of trouble by getting a mentor, a job, going to the library and reading, because when doing this you're never in trouble—you're active and have things to do. Without positive people, this world will not be the same; instead the modern world today would be a world of hate and hell, in which many would fail and not succeed in life.

"The Block," Janna Rae Nieto

He Motivates Me

Ashton Autry

The reason I'm not going to jail is because I want a career.
I see a lot of young, talented people going to jail. Because
they made some dumb choices. If I went to jail my dad
and mom would not be proud. My dad made some dumb
choices growing up, but luckily he got out of it. So, he
motivates me not to go to jail.

I Want to Do Good

Thomas Braswell

My brother is in jail. I don't want to go to jail because I want to do good. And not do drugs because they are bad. My dad's been in and out of jail. I want to go to college. And get a good job.

As Long as I Got My Mom

Jaylynn "One Jay" Nelms

My dad is in jail but I feel like he
needs to be in there. He did
something bad. I want him to know
that I love him and forgive him.
But me and him could never have
a good relationship ever.

Now, my dad is not a bad person, he just
made a bad mistake. Everybody
asks me if I am okay that he
is in jail. I always say yes because
I hide my feelings.
I know it's going to be hard growing up
without a dad. Kids who grow up
without a dad are more likely to make
bad choices, but as long as I got my
mom I am going to try to stay in school
And be good.

I Have Hope

Jaylin Ramos Arteaga

I'd like to discuss how we grew up. Children who come from immigrant families experience so much. Just imagine losing a parent or a loved one all of a sudden to forced deportation. What comes to mind is stress, anxiety, anger, and sadness. Imagine growing up with those feelings throughout your life, just to think about losing them one day. These are the effects of deportation. I have three siblings with two immigrant parents. We have all experienced anxiety, aggression, sleeping disturbances, depression, and trauma. Trauma is a big one that has affected us in many ways. I know of many and can also relate the experience of academic struggles and family dissolution. If you have been through something similar, you are not going through this on your own. The camps and systems are being handled so wrong. I have hope things will change.

"Waves," Alba Navas

White Lights in Dark Rooms

Elena Bernardez

I live in a doorway
Between heaven and hell
Where the devil and god have their own space
Hell has bodies all over the room
Souls sucked up like a vacuum
Dreams and memories gulped like blood

Shadows of darkness
Fear of being burned alive
With no flowers
Your son too scared to see you flat underneath the
tombstone

Darkness in me around my chest
Inside my eyes
I see the dark forest
Everything else leaves
But the darkness tries to escape
Release itself
So it could look for the next souls to haunt for life
Ancestors guide me
But I won't listen to them
They try to tell me there is something right behind
you

In the other room heaven
Has a big cross up in the ceiling
To keep hell from entering their home
Waterfall of holy water in the middle of heaven

Healing
Trust life
Strong and kindhearted.

When We Were Kids

"Childhood," Janna Rae Nieto

Incarceration Affection

Jennifer Birstein

How has my mom's incarceration affected me?
Imagine losing your mom at 3
Not to death but to the system
It was her fault, she's not a victim
She lacked wisdom
Yes, I was mad
But mostly sad
She missed most of my life
Left my dad without a wife
Pain cut deep like a knife
You aren't just affecting yourself when you go to jail
Think about your actions before you fail
You will prevail
We're tired of speaking to you thru the mail
We can't always afford your bail
You might not realize but you're setting a trail
You must lead the way
We value what you do and what you say
All we can do is pray
You made your bed but you don't have to lay
You don't have to stay
You can change
We believe in you even if you don't
Isn't that strange
You're now free
So do better for me

Sagrado Corazón de Jesús

Angela Fajardo

I ran to that room I knelt to that image
The red tile floors
On my knees

Tears flowing down
Feeling the blood in my lips
Feeling the edge of the tooth or the teeth

The praying began
The mourning for the loss
The crying starts
"Sagrado Corazón de Jesús en vos confío"
My heart of Jesus my trust is in You
My blond blue-eyed Jesus

"May my mom not spank me, not that hard"
I should have listened
But the drive was greater
The idea in my head won

Here was my plan
Standing on the handles of the rocking chair
I visualized the flip
I saw myself flying in the air
Flipping and landing on my feet
And at the end I gracefully bowed to the crow

So here it goes
Left foot on the left armrest
Right foot on the right armrest

I rocked back and forth, back and forth
Then I launched myself forward
And then the flip
The flip
The flip did not go well
The flip did not happen
Landed
Landed on my front teeth
The red bricks took the pieces away
Good-bye to my front teeth

The mouth burned
The lips bled
And I knew
Oh . . . No. . . .
I knew
I shouldn't have done it
My plan did not work

And here I was
Kneeling before my blond blue-eyed Jesus
"Sagrado Corazón Jesús en vos confío"

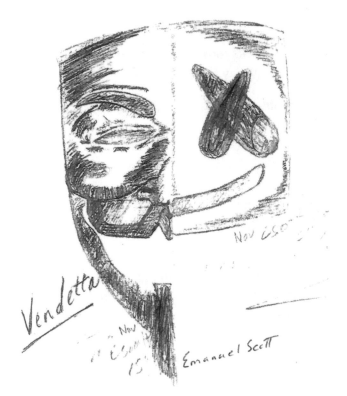

"Vendetta," Emanuel Scott

Hot Pink Razor

AG

I remember as a kid I had a scooter. I used to ride it up and down the concrete sidewalk and always ended up having scrapes on my ankles. I used to be a clumsy child so I got bruises and bled everywhere.

I used to have a hot pink Razor, and I used to love riding it.

Pretend

Daniel

Red velvet with pink polka dots
blond hair with a painted face
I play with a Barbie, who would have thought
Beginning to hide, my heart started to race
No one can know, the show must come to an end
Fall in line, and play the game called Pretend.

Down a Slope

Sarah Avalos

Down a slope I chased after a ball
cracks in the asphalt making me trip
the happiness I felt
playing with my best friend
was quickly ruined by pain
and the flow of red
down my leg.

Voice in my Head

King

If I'm being honest
there's a voice in my head I befriended.
I don't know his name yet,
this voice in my head.
Slightly disoriented but loud? I don't know.
There's this voice in my head saying I'm better off dead.
Sometimes I choose to agree with him,
say maybe he's right. See, this voice in my head
drives me crazy the louder he gets,
but the crazier I get, the more I understand.
See, this voice is a simple shadow behind a mask,
the same mask that I hide behind. And I find it funny
when I try to cope with myself. I also find it funny how
I put the others ahead, while the idea of putting lead in
my head
sounds quite diverting.
See, I have a silver pen with red ink
and a rose beige canvas.
I don't see what the issue is
To retaliate against his misuse.
Maybe it's the overwhelming voice in my head
which never reveals itself,
portraying itself as a friend,
but it only comes in silence.
When the beating of my heart becomes louder
how it thrills me.
Like did you know there is in the middle of Antarctica

Something like the size of Maine?
Just thinking about that makes me wonder
if Antarctica knows what it's like to be human.

Coloring Books

Jax

Crayons, pencils, pens and markers
Any toddler would go bonkers
When I wanted to draw a dog I said
"Mommy, I wanna draw a barker!"

Coloring books were so fun to color
Because it helped me recover
Happy is yellow, sadness is blue
Blue is the color I always used.

"Hope," Rah-San Bailey

Haiku

Hayden Brown

Social justice laws
U.S.A. just don't get it
land of the locked up

"The Monsters Under My Bed," Hiromi Maeda

young Criminal

Katherine Secaida

Mugshots had me feeling like a sad model
I was outshining my silver handcuffs
My fingerprints were bleeding through paper
I was giving out my signature
My dignity was no longer representing my name
But a number of charges

"Eye See You," Anonymous

I miss you

Stacie Ramirez

I miss your skin. Its softness, how smooth it was, how perfect your body temperature felt in my arms. I miss looking at you and wondering how it's possible to be such a beautiful small little human filled with so much love and energy. I miss looking at you with the desire to learn everything I possibly could about you. I miss how my lips felt against your cheek. I miss how full my heart felt when I held your little body in my arms. I felt like floating every time I saw you smile. I felt like the luckiest person in the world when I heard you laugh. I'd do anything for one more kiss, one more hug, one more word, just one more memory, with a smile, another laugh, just another moment by your side. So that I'm able to breathe again, because without you it feels like I have no reason to keep going. "You don't know what to live for until you know what to die for," they say. Well, I learned that you are my reason to live and my reason to die. Like nothing, I'd give up my life for you, because you are the best thing I've ever had.

"Ancestors," Janna Rae Nieto

Disorder in the House

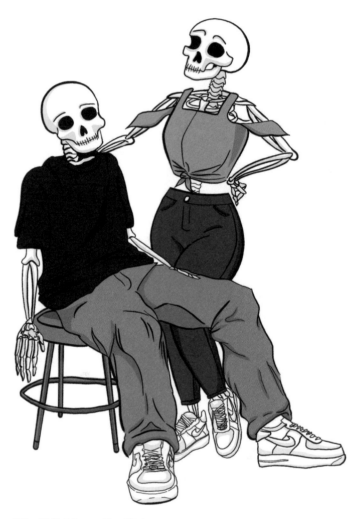

"The Talk," Janna Rae Nieto

Living in Los Angeles

Maricela Romero

Living in LA wasn't always the best. You see, life through my eyes would scare a square to death.

Poverty, violence, murder, never a moment to rest.

Fun and games are few but treasured like gold.

To most people living in LA is white picket fences, shopping Rodeo Drive, or cruising Hollywood Boulevard at night.

But me?

Every day is watching my back. Staying alert. Trusting nobody.

Life ain't always cupcakes and sprinkles, and you'd be damned to believe it is.

Truth is, my LA is going to sleep to the song of ghetto birds.

Whole families bang. Every other week it's a new funeral.

It's not all bad. Growing up in the hood has its advantages. You grow up faster; you get more respect. Walking down Lincoln Boulevard is an adrenaline rush because you feel untouchable. Of course, that's how you can end up dead.

I love LA. That's unquestionable. But I can't wait to leave. To go somewhere where there's constant rain, unlimited forests, maybe a lake.

Someplace like Oregon or Washington State.

Someplace safe.

"Singularity Tear," Kennedy King

Something I Never Talked About

The students of Steelton Highspire POPS club

Something I never talked about is that I share most everything in my life with my bestie, but I never talked to her about my dad being out of my life for a long time. He's back in my life and I'm still sad. My bestie doesn't know this.

Something I never talked about is that I go back and forth with myself a lot. "Don't wear this. You'll look fat." "You shouldn't say that." "Don't do that." I fight over what I wear because I will feel fat or ugly. I get really pessimistic and doubtful. I can become self-conscious and stressed because of it. It might be something stupid, but I don't mean to or even want to be this way. I try to convince myself that it's fine, but sometimes I just can't.

Something I never talk about is that I am always on edge about what people will think about me. I am afraid someone will not like the way I am and how I act. I never talked about this before because people will think it is for attention. I am afraid I will not be accepted as myself.

Something I never talk about is my home life. People don't have any idea what I go through, what I see and the things I endure. I feel hopeless. I feel worthless. I feel like I am at the bottom of a well and I will never climb out. I wonder why God has allowed me to go through what I do. This is something I never dare talk about. Even people who know there are problems don't know how bad they really are.

Something I never talk about is this—I love Piggies!

Something I never talked about is how no matter what I do in my life, I never feel like it is good enough. I feel like I will never be enough for anyone and anything.

What I Want My Parents to Know but Won't Tell Them

John Bembry

Growing up I realized I used to love you unconditionally before you showed your true colors.

Now I feel as cold-hearted as you, like father like son, right?

There're a lot of things I couldn't tell you only because you never cared or listened to begin with.

Even though I lived with you my whole life, you would still forget my birthday.

All the time you complained about the trash and dishes, I did chores daily and never got credit.

After what happened to my mom, seeing how you feel really killed me inside. Makes me feel like I don't even have a father.

You let your only daughter and my only sister alone to fend for herself in this cold world.

Now look what happened, my only big sister lying lifeless in a hospital bed.

Heartbreaking that you have her ashes and never cared. She is probably just somewhere in your closet.

Even though I don't really know my parents or my grandparents, or any family really, I do know what real love is. I've felt it and given it.

What made you neglect us and our love?

When I love, I love hard, and not feeling loved by my father made me seek it elsewhere, from other people.

With or without the love and support from you, I won't give up until there's no more air in my lungs.

I Hate School

Perry G.

I hate school
But I ain't no fool
Cause my grades drown like
They in a pool
So, wish me luck
Because every test I take
I get stuck
So, from on I'm going to rely on
the Lotto for a few lucky bucks

"Portrait," Chris Wright

Poem

Juliana Pinn

High school, a bittersweet memory
Filled with happy memories
   classes
   games
   friends
Friends, the ones who you trust to empty the pains of
one's heart
People who you trust
But sooner or later their true colors leak out
   Stabbing
   Scratching
   Tearing
   Your heart, no more a bright soul
   no more

"In the Room," Chris Wright

Against All Odds

Reggie Love Hurd

Against all odds my father's seed met my mother's egg.

Against all odds the egg that was me made it down the tubes into her uterus.

Against all odds the fetus that was me developed and took shape.

Against all odds, seven months later I came into this world.

Against all odds, I gained enough weight to finally go home with my mom.

Against all odds, I survived being picked on in elementary and in middle school for being skinny, or boney.

Against all odds, I made it through being a teenage alcoholic in high school. It wasn't easy to gain weight but it was easy to escape.

Against all odds, I survived jumping out of a moving car as a young adult. That bus just missed me.

Against all odds, I met the right people at the right time; they were in my path and they helped me when I was hopeless and loveless.

Against all odds, I'm here today to give hope to the hopeless and to give love to the loveless. Now I stand in a path to help others.

Put Yourself in My Shoes

Anonymous

Imagine that you have a very bad connection with your siblings. You were separated from both your sisters. One is in foster care. She lied about your mother and called the cops to come to the school. The other lives with your dad and you rarely get to see them. Your mom barely wanted your older sister because she wasn't your skin tone. And mom has anger issues. She would beat you up because you did something wrong, and your brothers are different. Your 11-year-old acts like the sister in foster care, and your youngest brother gets babied to the point he doesn't listen.

Instead, you get yelled at for all your brothers' and sisters' mistakes. Your grades are terrible, you're struggling, and you ask for help, and you still don't get it.

Then your nana dies, and you really don't have a connection with her—just like your siblings. You feel like she was always mad at you, and the saddest part, I don't even have a picture of myself with her.

"Women," Janna Rae Nieto

my Father's Addiction

Katherine Secaida

There are times where I see my father's addiction in two
    ways
Comprehending why he's an addict and knowing he will
    never change
My father's addiction is also my addiction
Accepting and denying
My father is in denial
I have accepted my father's addiction
When I was younger I didn't deeply ponder his addiction
I thought it was normal to have substances around
I would weep for my dad
As I grew older I realized addiction is intoxicating to
    deal with
My father's addiction taught me that love does not
    always win
I have to live with the pain and see my own father die of
    his obsession
Addiction is scary and inexplicable
Addiction taught me it's more natural to lose someone
    you love to something you don't cherish
It's confusing being the daughter of an addict
I love my father. I will do anything for him
That's where I get hurt
To do anything for an addict and get zero in return
To get laughed at when explaining to him how his
    addiction has traumatized me
My father is an addict and that's okay.

Sorry

Nelson Mendez

Dear Mother Nature,
We took advantage of you
Of your natural resources
Of your earthly, enjoyable ecosystem
Of your everything
I'm sorry.
Yet I shouldn't
Be the only one apologizing.
All the world's leaders,
Celebrities,
Companies,
And our President
Should be the ones who have to say,
"I'm sorry."
What have we done to help?
Ban plastic bags?
Check
Ban plastic straws?
Check
Ban plastic?
"Sorry, no thanks."
This is the response we get
When we are trying to
Create change,
Change that is barely occurring,
Change that only my generation
Cares about.
I don't know what else to say

When our planet is rotting away like a log in the
forest
And the older generation
Doesn't care about their nation
And no one is doing anything
But saying,
"I'm sorry."

"In the Beginning," Ellie Perez Sanchez

Trauma

Anonymous

When I think of traumatic experiences, I have had a lot. Most recently, just imagine my life. Your sister is pregnant and is due soon. She's 17. You are stressed and have experienced many feelings at once, when you really sit to think about it. You can be in a panicked state when you forget for a moment that this baby is coming in three weeks. But at the same time, you are happy. And scared. And sad.

It's good to try to control it all so you don't overwhelm yourself and you don't reach your personal limit that everyone else has. It gets worse and then it gets better as time goes on. I have no control over it, but I can handle it all and get through it all with my little happy face.

That's how I get through the traumatic experiences.

"Split," Anonymous

The Real and the Imagined

"Point of View," Nicole Bezerra

"The Days Unraveling," Nicole Bezerra

Family Visit

Karen Arellano

In September I had my first family visit with my dad after 22 years of his incarceration.

I was checked in along with two other women, and we walked together toward the family visiting rooms. We were each directed to a room, but while my neighbor was being checked in, I opened my gate and walked in. As the officer walked toward me, he asked me if my gate was open. I replied yes, and he said it wasn't supposed to be open. I began to feel skeptical about my surroundings so I said, "Hold up, is there someone in there?" The officer laughed and assured me that no one else was in there as he locked me in.

It felt like a kennel for humans. I briefly wondered if this was what it felt like to be my dog, Junior.

This officer was nice. As I pushed my custodial cart along the path toward the visiting room door, I couldn't help but notice everything that was wrong with the place. The sound of my cart made me feel sluggish, and in the spots where there was supposed to be grass, there was nothing but dirt.

I opened the door and left it wide open. I entered the place before putting my stuff inside to verify that there was no one else in the room. It was dirty, stained, unkempt, and I didn't feel comfortable touching anything. To make the place look nicer I unpacked my supply box and neatly laid all the dried food on the table. At least it added color. I unpacked my clothes and neatly placed these on top of my cart so that the place felt a little more livable, a little more like home.

I was excited to show my dad movies I'd seen between 2018 and 2019. I couldn't believe the prison had them. When I was finished setting everything up, I sat down on the "dining chair" that was directly facing the door. I waited with the door wide open until my dad was brought to me. When my dad was finally brought in, he walked over to me with the biggest smile. He hugged me and gave me a kiss on the cheek. He looked around with his big smile and excitedly said, "This place is nice!"

Royal Rebel

Elena Bernardez

Why don't you dress me as a pretty princess
Who never gives up and doesn't quit?
Royal rebel
Courageous enough to save someone under the train
Untie them from the train track before the train comes fast

Royal rebel
Serves her country
Feeds her people
And offers them jobs and a home in a five-star castle
And gives the village invitations to my 19th birthday
    masquerade ball to
Raise money for the school playground

Royal rebel storms the government and starts a union
With the servants to demand protection and body armor for
The war against our beliefs

Sun of freedom rising up to warn people
That there's a war and how we need our men
To suit up and fight for our people
Daughter of peace stops the war and
Tells them can we stop hating on each other and start
    forgiving
Children of unity
Dream big and bold

The Two Fridas
(inspired by the painting of Frida Kahlo)

Donaji Garcia

Out of all the paintings in the world, *The Two Fridas* is the one that I feel most connected to.

My everyday life has been like that painting, as if every morning I had to start all over again, the same lines and vibrant colors expressed throughout a simple photograph.

An evidence of there being two of me, two versions completely divided.

A part of me is passionate and is living life at its fullest. The romantic dancer who adores her culture as she dresses in the clothes of a Oaxacan dancer, like *el traje del Istmo de Tehuantepec*, and another day wearing the *traje of Éjutla de Crespo*. One who wears makeup and is mostly devoted to her love of folklore. A confident me who demonstrates to her family the love she has and the singing that lives in her soul.

In this world, she speaks Spanish with *admiración y respeto* always.

And I envy her. Although we are made to be there for one another, I do.

The other is different. She worries about what will come the next day and the day after. She is scared about each surgery and every hospital visit to the doctor, because she never knows if her sister will still be with her or not. She cares about her education and is terrified where the horizon will take her. The past was so full of pain.

Dance is when I breathe. It is my ice cream on summer days, and it has been the greatest adventure during my time in high school.

Thanks to dance, my heart pounds faster. And the two versions of myself are my reward.

Six-Word Memoir

John Bembry

The Journey Makes the Dream Reality

"Let's Dance," Hiromi Maeda

What If This Life Didn't Cost a Thing?

Mya Edwards

What if this life didn't cost a thing?
No rent to pay,
No gas to feed the car,
Buy groceries, what's that?
Homelessness wouldn't even exist.
Affordable housing?
I can achieve each dream and put all my energy into
creating something bigger than me.
But life is full of costs.
Love is free.
Dreams are free.
Nightmares are free.
But when you act them out or say them out loud,
that's when they cost a fortune.
Words are money.
Time is money.
Money is time.
Money is not free.
Work or freedom?
But work equals freedom.
Freedom means you have to work.
The wanting to be free only dooms you to work
harder than you really need to.
Who set the world up this way?
Capitalism?
Freedom fighters?

Congress?
The cost to live and the desire to live is up.
As confusing as it is to read this, that's how
confusing it is to understand the world we live in.
So what if we went back to trading goods and
growing things on our own?
Would we have more time to focus on our crafts?
Would we still be completely money driven?
Am I money driven?
Are we money driven?
Would our dreams have an easier time coming to life?
We would still be working hard, but in a different way.

What if this life didn't cost a thing?
No rent to pay,
No gas to feed the car,
Buy groceries, what's that?
Now we trade goods,
Our goods.
Homelessness doesn't exist,
There is no competition.
I can achieve each dream and put all my energy into
something bigger than me.
Everyone can be in first place with me.
Money will be a thing of the past.
Who agrees?

"Auto," Janna Rae Nieto

Roads to Freedom

"Eye in the Sky One," Janna Rae Nieto

"Eye in the Sky Two," Janna Rae Nieto

Forgiveness

Jennifer Birstein

Forgiveness is love
Love comes from above
When push comes 2 shove
Don't run
Don't hide
But don't let it slide
Let your emotions ride
It's okay 2 feel
That shows you're real
Let time heal
Go ahead 'n kneel
Say a prayer
He'll make a way
The sun will shine one day
2 be angry it's okay
Don't stay in the gray
Don't carry hate
You're 2 great
They need you
There's no debate
I know they messed up
But just forgive
Allow them 2 live
2 try again
Don't shut them out
Let them in
They need a friend
Just be there till the end
Just forgive

Stronger

Sofia Sanchez Annibali

Through a damaged mind,
to a broken heart,
From the hood known as the "j's"
and a family who struggles most days.
Where fights are common
and tears start flooding,
To pain so hidden,
and nothing's lifted.
From years of despair
and moments we'll never share,
With bad vibes
and silent rides.
Where love is never shown
and hate is most known,
You'll find a girl who is stronger alone.

"On Target," Janna Rae Nieto

A Summer of Firsts

Riva Goldman

It was the summer before my senior year in high school.
I expected a lazy summer hanging out with friends, but
it ended up being memorable in ways that I could never
have imagined.

One day, while I was home alone, blissfully listening to
the music of my favorite singer, everything changed. I got
a call from my best friend's father, informing me that my
father had been arrested, and even though I was sure that
it was a case of mistaken identity, he was guilty of the
crime that he was accused of. Shortly after the phone call,
two FBI agents showed up at our apartment; they seemed
uncomfortable, probably because I was alone, and I did
not know yet how bad the situation was. Then my father's
fiancée unexpectedly showed up, apparently intending to
get there before the FBI had. It wasn't until my younger
brother came home with a few friends that reality really
hit me. One minute my brother was smiling and happy,
then he was angry and disgusted with our father. Looking
at the scene from my brother's perspective, I saw how
bad it all looked, and I started crying. And so began my
summer of firsts.

I went to the federal courthouse for my father's arraign-
ment. For the first and only time in my life, I saw my father
wearing handcuffs. I sobbed uncontrollably in the courthouse. I barely ate for the first week after his arrest.

We went to visit him at the county jail for the first
time. We were pretty much first in line as we waited for
the doors to open to let in visitors. We quickly lost our
place in line when we walked into the area where visitors

are processed, because we were ignorant of how things worked for visitors. While we went to fill out a visitor's request form at a narrow table along the edge of the room, the experienced visitors rushed to the area where they handed in completed forms, since they'd filled out their forms while standing in the line. The next time we visited, we were much savvier. For the first of a handful of visits, I experienced talking to my father on a phone, separated by thick glass, just like in the movies.

Another first was a few days later, when I drove on the freeway alone in order to visit my father in jail. Before that day, I had always had an adult with me when I drove onto the freeway, and I was usually clenching the steering wheel in fear. But that day, I was relatively fearless, because I was determined to see my dad. While in line in the visitor's area, a seemingly nice man started to chat with me. I was naively making small talk with him when coincidentally a friend of my father's showed up in the visitor's line. He quickly sized up the situation, gave my new friend a certain look, and my new friend backed off. I had not realized that I had no business, as a 17-year-old girl, going alone to visit my father in jail.

The events that I'm describing took place decades ago. I have vivid memories of that summer and some of the people I encountered at the county jail. It was a horrific summer, but those events shaped my perception of myself and the world. I am still trying to understand why my father did what he did. I am grateful to everyone at POPS for recognizing that there are students who are dealing with the justice system and need a supportive place at school. Unfortunately, nothing like that existed when I was in school. I'm also grateful that POPS accepted me as a volunteer, because I am still healing.

Dear Freedom

Donaji Garcia

Dear Freedom,

Document your fragrance and mention my polytheistic tongue.

Oh my long-lost friend, whom I have not spoken to because you betrayed me fully,

And without knowing the consequences of your actions.

You come in the form of butterflies, crisp with energy eloping the conquered

Fire breathing through lanterns of prayers dancing the raven sweaters of linking arms

Cupped with courses of beauty in manacles giving its last show-and-tell

Gripped my innocence apart into this puzzle of time that quickly gathers its migration

With miles and miles distant I feel yet anguish at her sudden skin with bathing tattoos

Forgetting the tone of her skin or the person who she was before.

I have a love and hate relationship with you.

You grant to some access to your body and life when others just wait and wait

Until we stop and know you are not coming back.

Even though you know we are there, you leave us there at the sight of pain

Reciting verses of the Bible, hoping that my own family comes back to wherever she is now.

You have impersonated countless beings, which is in your favor because I could never look into your blue sapphire eyes again.

I declare that I fell in love with you, once upon a distance

When I was secretly admiring you, yet I didn't know what you did to the melody

Of sonnets and phrases both sacrificed in blood and life

Ancestors mentioned in textbooks and not her own mouth of tips and happiness

Blended with hormones and therapy sessions

Thanks to you.

I have yet to figure out why you did this: Out of all the nurturing

I gave you . . .

You pay me with these fallen dream catchers.

We spoke our secrets and wore matching bff bracelets

Ate chocolate chip ice cream accompanied with action movies

As we shared the same blanket of dismissing wonder.

And now . . .

Reality came as the roaring train without halting . . .

To tickle the clock . . .

As the newborn faith has yet to place her soul on my door.

Ringing the bell, reminding me that my past is chasing me

That the years are not passed in vain.

Don't feel bad, I forgive you.

I do.

I was locked and you let me out.

Breathing fresh air filled with the aroma of earth.

And soon enough, you will give her your bond as well.

Care for her as much as you did for me.

I just wish for her to fit into a category: family.

To be in those lines placed in that folder of my brain

Eternally, sentimentally ours.

To love and to share with the rest of my existence.

And for the butterfly to be transformed into the Statue of Liberty

Awaiting for others to see her

And know that Freedom really exists.

Sincerely,

Your Friend Who Cares

Transferring to a University

Katherine Secaida

There are numerous levels to grasp about my future. The steps are innocent but shift strongly and feel so unmanageable.

I was set to give up a semester of my education.

I stressed myself out. I did not want to give up a semester.

In the last week before school started, everything began to fall into place.

After I thought I was losing, I began to obtain what I craved.

I got what I was looking for.

Now I walk to the new world of a university and say good-bye to community college.

"Chillin'," Chris Wright

My Love for Reading

Brianna Carrington Myricks

My love for reading comes from my mother's side of the family. Every day I am grateful that my grandmother and mother passed this wonderful gift on to me. When I was in middle school, my mother bought me a book called *Wonder*, by R. J. Palacio. Every night I would read before bedtime. It was hard to stop talking about it to everyone at school, because it was an unforgettable novel. After I finished reading it, I realized that I had become addicted to books. I just could not stop reading. I read more because I enjoyed escaping this world and jumping into new worlds.

In high school, I began exploring different types of books: romance, historical fiction, mystery, and drama. Mysteries and dramas are my favorite genres. I prefer them because I like to imagine the characters solving crimes. I also want to know why each character chose to commit a crime. It is really fun to imagine the male characters, because I picture them as attractive.

My biggest challenge is to balance reading books for class and reading novels for fun. I often read two books at a time, switching back and forth depending on my mood. I always think about the book when I finish and believe I will always remember the stories' unforgettable endings.

I read when I want to spend time alone. While I am listening to pop music, I focus on reading and I don't notice the world around me. I also enjoy reading in public libraries because they are quiet, and I donate my books to them for others to enjoy. My family and friends admire my love of reading.

Listening to books on Kindle is a new joy, because I like hearing the readers act it out. I plan to continue reading for fun when I'm in college, because it is a part of who I am. My fear is that I am going to be busy with school and might not have much time to read for fun.

After college I plan to start a blog for teenagers and review teen crime novels. I want to give people advice on the best crime novels to read and how to balance reading books for class and reading books for pleasure while in high school. I want my followers to feel they can count on me.

I don't know what my future holds, but I can't give up reading. My dream is to pass this awesome gift on to my children and my children's children.

"Apples to Broccoli," Janna Rae Nieto

An Unchecked Box

Monserrat Hernandez

When filling out an application I come to the section that
invites multiple opportunities for discrimination.

You see, in this section there are always 5 boxes
5 main ones

Check the one that best describes you

Black
White
Hispanic
Asian
Other

Why is it that we can't see more than just our color?

Since day one we were assigned a box to check off
Whether it was used to describe our gender that led us to
become our own defender
Or to prove that it's not just our color that sets us apart
but that we can discover more about each other

You see, these boxes we are given are just labels,
Labels we are forced to live by
Although who we truly are is found inside of us
Your label shouldn't determine how high you will go in
life or how much you qualify
It shouldn't stop you from making your way to the top
and claiming your spot

You see, society always thinks it's
Us vs. Them
And Them vs. Us

Why do we let these labels cause such conflict and
division that doesn't allow us to see the world's vision:
That we all are equal
We must rip off these labels that keep us from feeling
incapable of being free
Because deep down we are meant to
connect and care for each other

No matter our gender, culture, or color
Labels are just that, labels
that keep us living and thinking in a world so small, it
doesn't allow us to recall that we are all
EQUAL.

Keep Us in Your Heart

"Hearts," Kennedy King

Against All Odds

Tinsae Yimer

Against all odds, I should know what I want to pursue.

A young girl, who moved from another country, wanting to know how to?

How to write what just might hold her truths.

I should make my parents happy and become a doctor or an engineer,

But against all odds of an immigrant child,

I want nothing that has to do with my insides or teaching a computer a certain input.

I want to live my life unashamed of the truth.

She Became a Human

Ellie Perez Sanchez

I don't wish to make you feel sad or anything
But I will tell you a sad story . . .
There she goes, thinking she can obtain the world with
just hope
There she goes, thinking she can achieve anything
without money
There she goes, thinking she can be better than stars even
without beauty
There she goes, thinking her bravery can only afford
force . . .

I don't wish to make you feel sad or anything
But I will tell you a sad story . . .
She's never known fear or sadness
But she knows triumph and courage
She's never known shame or envy
But she knows delight, victory, and pride . . .

I don't wish to make you feel sad or anything
But I will tell you a sad story . . .
You probably ask yourself why this is sad
But I will tell you
Even if in the present she thinks her life might be over,
It isn't—because even at 17 or 18, she doesn't know if she
can obtain the world

I will tell you a sad, human, common story
She never trusted before, and it was this . . .
What made her feel powerful,

What made her have control over feelings or becoming a
human
This is the sad story she loves the most
She fell in love
She fell in love, she fell in love
She fell in love
I mean, are you a human yet, can you relate?
She fell in love
She now feels
Not just love, but all the pain that comes with it
She's losing control now
Fighting the truth now
Trying to hide now
Trying to hold now

This is a sad story
Because remember, she has trust issues
She fell in love!
She's losing control now
Pain and trauma devour her inner peace
She let in!
He is now in
She's losing control now

This is the sad human story
Climbing mountains of feelings, going back down to . . .
feelings
But don't worry, she's now made peace with herself
She's now realized that being loved doesn't have to be
scary
She's now breathing like everybody else
From being that beautiful angel looking down on earth
Her eyesight and heart made her become a human

She is now aware of love
She now knows that every single little infinity with her
lover counts
But this is the sad story you can flap
Lover, you can ride because you've won the star of your
life, and who else cares?
I didn't make you think about that one person :)

"Close," Alba Navas

Scared for the Future

Tinsae Yimer

Will I be alone for the rest of my life?

I find myself occupying my brain with irrelevant thoughts and ideas just to stay away . . . because I'm afraid.

I often have good hunches about what is to come.

It's bad. Real bad.

I'm Looking for a New Heart

John Bembry

I'm looking for a new heart. Mine is damaged beyond repair.

It works sometimes or never, or when it wants to.

It doesn't do well with Anger. It will erupt like a volcano, burning friendships or itself.

It doesn't show too many emotions.

It feels cold in my chest and it tends to make me numb.

It seems to react to pain more than anything. Having a fun memory can trigger the pain it once had.

It enjoys darkness and solitude.

I've put a lot of work into it. It was almost completely broken.

Not sure if this is how a heart should feel.

If anyone has a heart and doesn't mind lending it, that would be great.

I can't physically take it, of course, but maybe it can mend mine into what it should be.

It takes so much willpower and focus on the future to not let it affect me mentally.

At least I know my mind is strong. As for my heart, it's going to take a lifetime of treatment to return it to normal. If it ever has been.

I just hope to feel true happiness one day.

"Open Heart," Anonymous

Things I Never Said

Judith Lopez

There are things I'd like to share with you.
Things that I am afraid to communicate.
Things that make me bite my tongue
As I long for the words to pour out of my mouth
The way honey drips effortlessly into a sweet cup of tea.
There are things I'd like to share with you.
Like the fear I have of feeling.
Of feeling all of these bottled-up emotions I hoped would
    wither away
Like the dandelion seeds in the summer night breeze.
The truth is, I am afraid to admit that I'm a little broken
Because I do not know how to open up without feeling
    judged.
Or how to feel without letting the pain in until my skin is
    paper thin.
Or how to cry without my tears feeling like acid pouring
    down my cheeks.
When I am feeling blue, I want you to hold me
Because I cannot find the words
To let you know that I am hurting.

Catch Me If You Can

Katherine Secaida

I feel empty with love
A lonely love
A lonely woman with love.

So much love I have given myself, and so much love
to give to you
But it's dark, and I'm screaming.
I'm underwater
You can't see or hear me
No one can
But everyone can see me.

The closer you swim into my water,
The higher it rises
And still
I feel lonely.

My face is underwater and I'd rather drown than see
your broken heart.

I am falling, and I just want to fall
I want to fall into the arms
I have been waiting for.

While I stand up straight, I see no one coming
When I fall, I land on a cloud, but I am ready to land
in your arms.

When I scream, I'm on top of the world
When I laugh, I'm in the dark

When I cry, I'm in the ocean
Every day I am slowly falling

I am looking over a cliff
Ready to jump into your arms.

An Autistic Athena

Donaji Garcia

Owl eyes speculate the fertile soil they walked on
And the goddess they had hidden in mind and spirit.
From the head of skill came the descendant
That brought life to the family she had.
Both hands set on the sky
Fingers touching each constellation they were to recall.
Beauty dancing on her cheek
And sparkled the smile of not an Aphrodite,
But someone who was the most natural form
Of an angel based upon a photograph or painting.
She couldn't speak, yet she would talk
With the language of her body and actions
Mesmerizing the myth
Bravery face-painted every once in a while
Sheltered by clouds of hugs
And olive trees break the necklace of time
Until I see her again . . .
Once more.

I've Been Experimenting

Mya Edwards

I've been experimenting with my life,
mixing emotions with tree and drink.

I've been experimenting with my love,
giving my heart to a woman was the biggest step.

I've been experimenting with my love,
imagining myself in different people's arms.

I've been experimenting with my love,
giving my heart and time to those who show and give
back the same effort and energy I give them.

I've been experimenting with my love
becoming friends with those I am interested in, revealing
my whole life to them.

I've been experimenting with my love,
picking and choosing who I welcome into my family.

I've been experimenting with my love,
sharing my anxiety and experiences.

I've been experimenting with my love,
not feeling obligated to give someone all my time but
taking time for myself.

I've been experimenting with my love,
being by myself, single.

I've been experimenting with my love,
resting when I'm tired.

I've been experimenting with my love,
going with the flow and doing what I feel at the moment.

I've been experimenting with my love,
not going through with plans that I've made.

I've been experimenting with my love,
I know what I want.

I've been experimenting with my love,
waiting, going with the flow, and not rushing love.

I've been experimenting with my love,
it takes time.

Saying Good-bye, Hello to Yourself

Yachi Bonilla

It's nice that you are still alive I've always wanted to talk
    to you since by now you should've been dead
As I notice you cry
Who knew hope could turn into hell
Wondering if the pain is still there
Wondering how I can stop feeling or wonder why I'm alive?
I have nothing to fear, but I could pick up a knife
Cut myself
Let my blood fall
Thank you for not killing me
I should introduce myself to my new life
How does it feel going to hell?
The visit was good
Would you rather be there since you're already dead?
How can I stop the people from crying
Or caring for you?
People have feelings
So try to live
When do you learn not to care
And feel pain-free?
So many questions that can't be answered
Taking it step by step
Not being addicted to seeing
My blood flow through the ground
How can you say this to people without looking stupid
    or crazy?
Sadly, that's how they're going to see you
But here I am, again alive

Almost Adults

"On the Lawn," Janna Rae Nieto

12th-Grader

Mya Edwards

Question after question / What the hell is my life?
Am I gonna be the human that I want or am I gonna think
twice?

I am unstoppable / Probable / Always psychological /
Reasonable / Stubborn / And other times unforgivable /
I'm growing up and I can't change that / I can't turn back
the clocks / So I question all the "what if . . . ?" facts / I'm
always in the counseling office with questions that I need
answers to / fast / And I ain't mad at myself because I'm
preparing for my greatness.

I am unstoppable / Most times unforgivable / Senseless /
Emotionless / Or too emotional / And always
psychological / I'm growing up and I don't want to change
that / I can't turn back the clock so I rather just have a
ball and make a good time of anywhere that I'm at / I find
the good in funerals, family kickbacks, and barbeques that
you need to wear rain caps at. . . . Ha, I choose to have a
good time wherever I'm at.

I am unstoppable / Probable / Always psychological /
Reasonable / Solving / Striving to be unpredictable /
Senseless / Emotionless / But mostly emotional /
Stubborn / A lover / A fighter / A queen /A biter /
A king / Changer / A bundle a fire / But always
psychological.

"Mushrooms," Janna Rae Nieto

A moment I Want to Forget

Bamlacktsega Haile

There was a moment when my mom went crazy. It was a Friday night, the anniversary of my brother's and father's deaths. People had come over to our house to support my mother, but something triggered her mind, and she was yelling and trying to hurt herself.

Nobody could calm her down, and I was afraid. I didn't know what to do. I ran to her and held on for dear life. If it weren't for me, I don't know where my mom would be right now.

I never want her to lose me, because she's been through so much in her life, and I don't want to cause her more pain. I hate talking about this because every time I think about it, I go to a bad state of mind. I try to forget, but sometimes, when I'm alone, it crawls back into my mind.

I Am Who I Define Myself As

Erika Hernandez

My biggest fear is being nothing in life, being another disappointment and living check to check and being angry at the world. Being the youngest of four, I know who I want to be. I crave being the first one to be someone. I see the way my parents view my siblings with such sorrow. I can't and won't carry that kind of weight. I wish to prove to everyone that I will be able to carry my own weight. The satisfaction of proving everyone wrong who said I can't be anything in life is my biggest craving in life.

Immature People

Ellie Perez Sanchez

When they think of teenagers "ugh immature people"
They say we're reckless and useless
Making stupid excuses
But there's a lot on our mind,
So much behind
Stressed out
But it is always "fine"
They sometimes ask
But we can't describe
They say we're dramatic, that we're just overreacting
Immature because we just don't wanna talk

When they think of teenagers "ugh immature people"
They say we're reckless and useless
Making stupid excuses
We know more than what we tell you
But can't always put into words
We feel more than what you see
We know you say depression might just be a branch of
      the teenage years' tree
We don't cry because we want to
But you'll assume it's because she's another 18-year-old

When they think of teenagers "ugh immature people"
They say we're reckless and useless
Making stupid excuses
We're not crazy romantics, but we still know what a heart is
And when it's cracked, it also hurts, burns
The pressure, the hesitation, hurts, burns

The don't-miss-out, the can't-fit-in, hurts, burns
The building-back-when-we're-in-pieces-and-pieces-
    again, hurts, burns
The thinking-overthinking-quite-a-lot, hurts, burns
The splinters you put in when you tell us something,
    hurts, burns

But when they think of teenagers "ugh immature people"
They say we're reckless and useless
Making stupid excuses
They say age will cure it all
They assume we think we know it all
But we just want to catch up and explore it all

"Women's March," Hiromi Maeda

See You Later, City of Angels

Katherine Secaida

The ocean breeze won't sing in my ears
The sunsets at the beach with their artistic colors won't
    decorate my body
The warm hot chocolate from Alana's coffee shop won't
    reach my lips
The helicopter roaming in my neighborhood won't shine
    its light into my windows
The edges of my childhood home won't tell me stories
As it rained on my last night in LA, City of Angels,
My past washed to my feet
I kissed the rainy midnight and said good-bye

Christmas

Jennifer Birstein

It's Christmas, why aren't you sober?
Things are getting clearer
Now that I'm getting older
Pains hitting me like a boulder
Thoughts saying be stronger
Can't hold on much longer
Makes me wanna cry
But tears won't come down, why?
When I confront you, why do you lie?
Why are you getting high?
Why are you on?
Why are you sprung?
Why are you addicted to this drug?
I thought it would be peaceful now that you're free
But nothing will ever be perfect, I see
Now Papa's screaming
Because Nana doesn't want you leaving
You are so deceiving
What's the meaning?
Wake me up—wait, I'm not dreaming
I did your hair
But you did nothing for me
You were never there
But I still care
It's okay, Mama, go to sleep
While everyone deals with this pain so deep
You go to the bathroom and do drugs and creep
But we all see

You see what you reap
At least I'm spending time with you
Even though wrong is all you do
Maybe one day you'll be sober and my dreams will
come true

Death of a Teenager

John Bembry

17. Graduated with more confidence than ever. Yet so many obstacles I will face that start with where I lay my face.

18. First telemarketing job to support my household, yet the occupation is not enough to satisfy without criticism.

19. First semester at Santa Monica College. The learning is different and changes are happening, yet some things stay the same.

20. New job, new semester, new chances. New opportunities. Yet I'm belittled and told to pursue a trade.

21. Finally legal, ready to use what I've learned in life for life. Yet when life hits hard, I'm hearing only all of his problems: All five of his children are anchors, and we're the cause of his being underwater.

22. Unsocial, unstable, and left with the scar on my hand to prove the loss of restraint. Yet I try to keep love in my heart, God in my mind, and success in my future.

23. Defeated the demons of my teenage life, ready to find love and settle down. Yet when life hits hard I'm hearing the same things again. But worse. Never will I hate or belittle my child. Never will I make him feel like nothing, and never will I let him feel or go through any of these things alone.

24. On November 18, 2019, I will celebrate my first birthday with no family member involved and no real place to call home. Yet that little fire of hope and faith continues to burn and fuel the confidence I need to get through another day and be my best.

my New Best Friend

KS

LA, California. Venice High School. Freshman year, entering an all-gender bathroom.

All I hear is laughing in the stalls.

Smoke everywhere.

I see my homegirls come out with heavy eyes, dark red eyes.

One looks at me and says, "Wassup, Kat." She coughs as she says my name.

My other homegirls keep laughing and giggling and I'm thinking, "They're high."

One of them says in a monotone, "Hey, you wanna take a hit?"

I make a face, saying, "Ummm, I'm not sure."

But I took this pen-looking thingy into the stall. My heart racing, sweaty palms. I kept staring at the pen. Once I took a hit, I started coughing so bad, like holding my breath underwater, as if my lungs were being deprived of oxygen.

My homegirls say, "Woah! You okay there, Kat?"

I just can't stop coughing and I start to laugh. I clear my throat and say, "Yeah, I'm fine."

After lunch, I walk out of the bathroom. I don't even remember how long I was sucking on that thing. My eyes feel tired, my mouth dry, my heart racing so fast, and I'm thinking, "Holy crap, I'm so high."

Throughout Spanish class I felt paranoid. I kept laughing for no reason. I was seeing things honestly, and that was the best feeling ever.

I had been stressed the past few weeks with my schoolwork, and this pen took it all away.

Not worrying about anything, thinking I was going to get caught by my Spanish teacher. This was really freaking me out, as if I was playing hide-and-seek and I didn't want anybody to know where I am.

I didn't want her to find out that I was high.

After school my stomach was crying bad, so I went into the fridge. I started to chop down the food. It tasted real good. This was my really happy place. Mixing up foods. I didn't I care. I was just so hungry. I ate eggs and avocadoes together. Hot Cheetos and milk. Best combination ever.

All by sucking down that smoke from that pen.

Everything dissolved. Didn't have to deal with my mom or dad telling me what to do.

This became my happy place.

Love these feelings that make the world a better place.

I have my own pen now, so when my parents go to sleep, I close the living room door, play some Dr. Dre or some '90s music.

Then . . . just smoke away.

Can't ask for anything else.

That pen became my best friend.

"Malibu Moon," Reggie Love Hurd

The Broken Bowl Project

Steelton Highspire Broken Bowl Project

Steelton Highspire POPS Club

These broken bowls represent us as individuals; we are vessels that hold many things. But sometimes we break and need to be put back together.

Our brokenness changes us, makes us who we are. And so the painting on the outside of the bowl represents who we are on the outside, and the words on the inside of the bowl express all the hidden components that make us us.

The inside of the bowl is reserved for words that describe what pieces of ourselves that shard represents.

Not all the pieces will fit together perfectly. There will be some that got lost or turned to powder when the bowl was broken.

We were patient as we reassembled and we problem solved. Just as in life, not everything goes the way we always planned.

Sometimes the most significant parts of the bowl are the gaps where the piece was too broken to be mended. For many people this represents a deep wound from our past and may be especially hard to talk about.

We used glitter and sparkle to highlight our cracks, because we believe in POPS club and that these gaps are an important part of who we are and why we meet in our group each week and grow.

"The Steelton Highspire POPS Club Bowls"

Seven Years Ago Today

"Vulgar," Jason Cruz

Seven Years Ago

In 2014, the first POPS the Club anthology, *Runaway Thoughts*, was published, featuring work by the students of the very first POPS club at Venice High School in Los Angeles.

The pieces that follow were first published in that volume.

A Voice

Joey Estrada

No place has even been home for long. Nomadically moving from city to town and back was the nature of my childhood. Just because my ID says that I am an adult does not mean that I have control over my life. Thinking that life back in Los Angeles as an adult meant stability in that way was wrong, but simply accepting it has made life easier.

Looking back on my life now, it seems that every small move was an upgrade from a bad situation to a better one. Yet, as an "adult," I am not sure if it was just the hopeful optimism of a child wanting a better life. The earliest memory I have is of crawling around on a dirty brown carpet that inhabited our living room floor. It was a small home, but its backyard inspired my young mind to play when I was alone. However, living with my mother meant living with her and whoever she had gotten tangled up with at the time.

I met my real father when I was in kindergarten. He was sent to jail when I was an infant. His crime was trying to strangle my mom. He was high on crack at the time—he became addicted when I was born. I remember not asking, "Where's my daddy?" but saying to my mom, "I want to see my dad." At that point I had no memory of seeing his insanity and simply wanted to meet him. And I did. There are definitely fond memories of seeing him after he cleaned up. He was an intensely bright man, capable of making people smile wherever he was, teaching me wherever he could, and showing me that life is a lot what you make of it.

After moving away and back the first time, my dad and I still had a good relationship. Stranger was the fact that he had a friendly relationship with my mother. Then I remember her meeting someone on vacation, and I remember her going to visit him once her vacation ended. She always seemed to rush into a relationship for my sake. Learning that shocked me, but sadly it made sense.

We lived in Washington State for seven consecutive years, my mother and I slowly experiencing the mistake of jumping into one bad relationship to escape another. My mom was able to separate from him, and we are now living comfortably with my grandma in Venice, but it's just another stepping stone.

My dad died shortly after I moved back to California. After having not seen him for most of my life, we were finally reconnecting. I was planning to see him at my high school graduation, and I was so looking forward to it. After all, he'd made it to my kindergarten graduation.

I don't remember the last words I said to my father, but I do remember his voice. Writing is an opportunity for me to make my own voice memorable so that one day I can communicate with others—if only my own children—in the way that my dad communicated with me.

Living Poetry

John Bembry

The pain in me is nowhere compared to the
Pain of the prison system.
The way I speak, you should know each and every one of
my feelings.
I smile at the reader, but frown at the ceiling.
I'm one man, that's out of a million.

Never going to prison is something I had envisioned
My Number One objective, like a military mission.
Disciplined, remember my life as detention.
Crippin', killin', now, I'm just chillin'.

People say I'm quiet, but when I talk they don't listen.
I love new beginnings. I had bad endings.
Friends turn to enemies but asking for forgiveness,
I would never be the same if I go to prison.

Same thing every day, I see no difference.
2 Pac died for this. Heavy metal empty clips
Rappin' is my passion. It's considered as a gift

That I could make a meaning using all my intelligence.
So when you judge Black, just remember this,
Wise in his eye, plus smart within the creases,
Pain of the prison system, life or death comparison.
Rags to riches and it's poverty to lavish men.

Scavengers are savages and vultures are carnivorous.
I never do poetry because I'm always living it.
Incarcerated people, most of the indigenous
Doin' what I do, don't like it or you feeling it.

Drugs

Kei'Arri McGruder

Drugs are the only happiness in some people's lives.

You may never know what their personal connection is with it.

It could be like a warm hug or a peace that fills the hole in someone's soul.

Funny to think of that—a hug from something as simple as a drug.

It kills the soul and the mind.

Some may use to erase the pains of yesterday or the fights of loved ones or the touch of a molester. A soft voice saying, *He will never be able to hurt you again.*

A way to escape from the world, from all the prejudiced ways, and shunning of the unknown and different.

It breaks up families and tears you apart from the inside out.

Drugs are like little hugs that make you feel loved, or even a little piece of joy.

But for what it's worth, I believe that drugs are just a simple substitute for what the soul has missed.

"Rain," Alba Navas

Godfather

Nelvia Z. Marin-Caballero

Seen him a few times
Just not enough to memorize his tattoos from head to toe
All that's left in my household are negative comments,
    with a bad vibe
A picture of a man about 5'9" holding a black gun
Their mouths saying, you won't see him in an office
    wearing a suit
But you will catch him behind bars, in jail, wearing an
    orange jump suit
Black numbers on the left side of his chest
Standing with concern, watching everything with eagle eyes
His wife started a new chapter in life
Leaving him behind

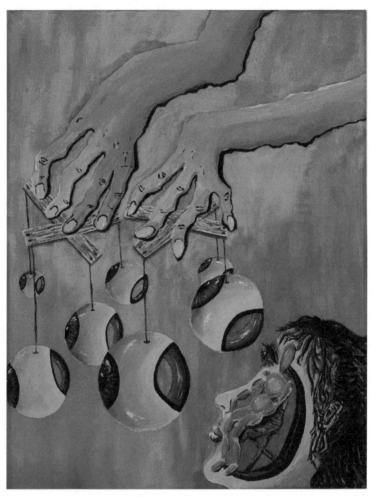

"The Lens Shown to Us," Nicole Bezerra

What Is Life?

Luis Nunez

I don't know what life is to you, but to me it's a test.
No loopholes, shortcuts, or secret passages.
It's not a bar or a quiz; it's a journey to success.
You might fail many times but you have to get up, try again.
Eighteen, struggling with my
Mom in sickness.
Sleepless nights in the hospital, trying to keep my faith.
Have a sister with
some cancer.
Have a brother in despair.
Met him once when I
was ten and never heard from him again.
In jail for ten years.
Yeah, he robbed and
took the blame.
Rose up with Dad who turned out to be a fake.
Left me at ten and
walked away
with no remorse to contemplate.
Soon found out my father was really dead.
All my life I was told that the dead man in the pictures
    was uncle.
What the f— is happening?
My mind is playing tricks on me.
I feel like it's a dream, but it's more like a nightmare.
I can't wake up. I'm
stuck.
All I can do is listen
to inspirational music and connect.

But all I want to do is disconnect.
If only I had a plug.
I don't really give
a f—.
But I'm not giving up.
Be 1 in 5 to graduate.
Because mom still has faith in me.
She sees success in me.
Wants the best for me.
Still believes in me.
Says my dad's in me.
I'm all that she has left.
She just hopes that I save her.
She doesn't want another black sheep or a bandit on
    the streets.
She tells me life isn't cheap.
Sh— was deep.
That's just my definition of what life may be. I'm not
speaking for anybody else.
This right here is for me.

"Vistas," Hiromi Maeda

Irreplaceable

Idalia Munoz

My brother comes home sometime in April. I've been picturing this day for a long time now. The last time he was out on the streets, he was my age, 17. Soon he'll be 21, out on parole and trying to get back on his feet. I'm afraid he'll do something that will send him back behind bars. My parents have suffered enough. They don't need more stress.

The worst thing was seeing my dad cry every Thanksgiving and Christmas because his son wasn't home celebrating with us. My dad would go on and on about how much he messed up raising us, when that wasn't true. My brother happened to be a teenager trying to live his life with his friends and ended up getting himself into big trouble.

Every weekend my parents would visit him. For the first year of my brother Ulises' incarceration I was not allowed to visit because I was underage and the judge would not approve a special visit.

I remember the first time I visited my brother; it was the longest process ever. Not only did I have to wait in line for an hour, but that was followed by a 10-minute drive to a facility and then a 45-minute wait while they released him to the visiting room. I was excited to finally see him and give him a hug until my dad told me there would be a window between us and we would talk on a phone. At that moment I realized how screwed up things were.

I hate to admit it, but it was awkward speaking to him over the phone. He'd been gone for so long that I forgot what it was like to have a brother. I know it shouldn't be this way, but it is. It has been almost five years since he was sentenced, and a lot has happened in my life.

I hear the helicopters almost every night flying over my neighborhood searching for someone. And I fear when Ulises gets out, I will hear the helicopters and wonder if they are looking for him.

I've read that more than 50 percent of people who have been released from prison will return within the next three years. I don't want my brother to become another statistic.

Something has to change and will change when my brother comes home.

Visiting Day

Kei'Arri McGruder

I walk through the big silver doors,
Ready to be searched.

I'm only eight,
But I'm already used to being patted down
And suspected of breaking the law.

They think I may have a knife
Or a gun so they can try to break out and make a run

He takes his magic wand and waves it around to me
My turn is done.
I walk down the hall and I can feel all the negativity.

I see the faces of the blue men
Hoping for someone to come and love them.

I look up and see this tall man. I scream, "Daddy!"
I go up to the window and see his sad face.

experimenting

John Bembry

I've been experimenting, I've been around.
I've been lost and I've been found.
I've been through hell and back.
I've been broke and I've been with stacks.
I've been through drama, I've been in hospitals, injuries
    to me and my mama.
I've been defeated by my own conscience.
I've been victorious on other occasions.
I've been doing a little drinking and
I've been doing a little blazing.
I've been on and off probation.
Never going back to that life.
I've been planning to stay off and not thinking that twice.
I've been spending sleepless nights in the studio.
I've been chilling, rolling with criminals.
I've been victimized, I've been predator.
I've been over that, that's kiddie stuff.
I've been respected. I've been neglected.
I've been accepted. I've been rejected.
I've been alienated. I've been humiliated.
I've been working hard, I've been with my occupation.
I've been important, I've been nothing.
My whole life I've been turning nothing into something.
I've been mastering my artistic life,
I've been flirting, but waiting for my wife.
I've been the nicest person I know.
I've been expressing feelings people can't show.
I've been deep in thought, I've been rhyming.

I've been moving up, I've been climbing.
I've been treating other humans like diamonds.
I've been hurt, only on the inside I've been crying.
I've been experimenting with my life.

Listening

Alondra Magallanes

POPS isn't an ordinary club about robotics, math, religion, or sea creatures.

POPS is about prison.

My brother Ariel accompanied me to the first meeting of the club that meets in Room 120. We entered the classroom, grabbed a peanut butter and jelly sandwich, a cup of lemonade, and chocolate brownies—the best deep chocolate brownies. Then we sat in a circle and waited for more students to arrive.

At least 15 students showed up, probably more, and what happened over the next 25 minutes was not what I could have ever anticipated.

I thought I was alone when it came to prison.

My brother and I, who are usually quiet people, became surprisingly open and talkative. Ariel began pouring out his emotions. He couldn't stop. I followed.

And everyone actually listened. Almost everyone spoke openly about why they were there. Not everyone was directly affected by prison—a few came just for the food, which was fine because they all listened and understood some of what we felt when they heard our stories. Hearing my schoolmates' stories that first day made me realize I had taken for granted the time with my dad when he was a free man.

Talking helped me break out of my shell, helped me gain the confidence to try out for the drill team and helped me bring up all my grades.

I released the shame I felt about my relationship to prison. In that room students who never noticed each other on campus sat together and listened to each other. In that circle we acknowledged each other's talent in writing poems, essays, stories, and in music. The meetings brightened every Wednesday.

Over the next few months many speakers visited. Some of their stories made us cry or made us angry about what goes on inside prisons. Not every speaker expressed shame. Some regretted decisions they had made in the past. It was obvious that in one way or another, in the long run, their prison experience had made them better people. Now they worked twice as hard as they had worked before, just to get by. Some suffered great losses like the loss of a mother, being expelled from every school in the country, racking up huge legal bills, becoming homeless, and wasting years of their lives. One speaker explained how her life became so difficult she turned to drugs and alcohol and her sister attempted suicide multiple times, but now she and her sisters have become successful businesswomen and turned their loss and sadness into a nonprofit organization that helps women who have become victims of violence.

The club helped push me in the right direction mentally and emotionally, allowed me to make long-lasting friendships, and provided me with unforgettable memories. It filled me up on brownies and lemonade every Wednesday, and I'm grateful to those who listened to my stories and accepted my past. Most of all, I'm thankful for all that I've learned.

Author/Artist Bios

AG is a 16-year-old student at James Monroe High School. She and her sister are first generation Americans of her family, which came from Armenia looking for a better life.

Xavious Anderson is a POPS club member at Callaway Middle School in Georgia.

Sofia Sanchez Annibali is a senior at Venice High School who loves to dance, draw, write, and be creative in every form. Always looking for something new to learn or get better at.

Karen Arellano grew up in LA and is currently working on a bachelor's degree in political science with a minor in history from the University of California, Irvine. She has an AA in paralegal studies from West Los Angeles College. Upon graduating, she intends to pursue a juris doctor degree. As a person who has experienced the incarceration of immediate family members, she was drawn to POPS for its mission to transform the lives of youth affected by incarceration.

Jaylin Ramos Arteaga is a POPS club member and a senior at Lawndale High School in Lawndale, California. "I am 17 years old, I grew up in the city of Hawthorne. I enjoy dance and have been dancing since I was 6 years old."

Ashton Autry is a POPS club member at Callaway Middle School in Georgia.

Sarah Avalos is a senior at James Monroe High who loves video games and her friends.

Rah-San Bailey is a POPS club member at Venice High School in Los Angeles.

John Bembry is a 2013 Venice High graduate. POPS author. Inglewood artist. Never give up hope. Onstage he's SteezoThePlotter.

Elena Bernardez is a senior at Bronx Academy of Letters. She loves theater and poetry and wants to be an actress and a writer.

Nicole Bezerra is a POPS club alum and graduate of El Camino Real Charter High. "I love everything about art. It has the power to express anything and everything, it can make people think about what is going on in the world or what may be going on within themselves, it can bring people together whether it be one-on-one or globally, and I think that is so beautiful."

Jennifer Birstein has been part of POPS the Club since 2017. "I am on a journey of creative self-expression."

Blue is a 17-year-old with too many hobbies ("I may need therapy"). "Anyways, I love animals and my favorite color is depression blue."

Yachi Bonilla, a graduate of the Bronx Academy of Letters in New York City, is a writer and POPS the Club member.

Thomas Braswell is a member of POPS the Club in Troup County, Georgia.

Hayden Brown is a member of the POPS club at Culver City High.

Celine is just a high-schooler trying to get by.

Jason Cruz is a senior at Los Angeles High School of the Arts who enjoys graphic design. His artwork represents an abstract route to what POPS the Club means to him, and how he rates the prison system: Vulgar. "The system is a paradox and malevolent loop of bringing injustice more than justice to people of color, impoverished communities, and the wrongfully convicted. It is a problem I genuinely want to solve. I believe every single one of us is a center of a universe and can overcome issues that face us—no matter the scale, we have to build with honesty and solidarity."

Daniel is a student, an artist, and a poet.

Mya Edwards is a 12th-grader at Venice High School. "I am 17 years old; I write poetry, dance, and make jewelry."

Richard Anthony Espinoza is a senior at Culver City High School.

Joey Estrada is a Venice High School graduate who moved to Idaho in 2017. He currently works as an airframe/power plant mechanic for a large regional airline.

Donaji Garcia is a bilingual poet at Venice High School. She dedicates her work to Brianna Myricks, who has been her unconditional friend, and Catalina, her sister, who has shown her the importance of love and life.

Angela Fajardo, a native of Granada, Nicaragua, graduated from Garfield High School, where the legendary teacher Jaime Escalante was her teacher. She has a master's degree in bilingual/bicultural education from Loyola Marymount University and a doctorate in education from USC. She currently teaches Spanish at Venice High and is a POPS the Club supporter.

Riva Goldman is a volunteer at Venice High School's POPS club in Los Angeles.

Carter Gray loves writing and uses it as a form of self-expression.

Perry G. is a member of the POPS club at Santa Monica High School.

Ronald Griffis is a 17-year-old junior at Venice High School. He's grateful his mom has worked hard to make a better life for her family. He wants to work in a tech-related job when he graduates.

Bamlacktsega Haile is a member of the POPS club at Venice High in Los Angeles.

Morgan Hamilton is a member of POPS the Club at Culver City High School in Culver City, California.

Erika Hernandez is a sophomore at Venice High. She likes to write and spend time with friends and family.

Montserrat Hernandez has been a member of POPS the Club at LA High School of Arts in Los Angeles for three years.

Reggie Love Hurd has worked at Venice High School for four years as a paraprofessional. New to education, Reggie's passion is music and the arts, and that passion is used to inspire the children and mold young artists and writers.

Cierra Ingersoll is a writer who graduated from Venice High in 2014 and is a proud forever member of POPS the Club.

Julian Izaguirre is a member of the POPS club and a student at Venice High School.

Jax is living in a spectrum of surrealism.

Jazmin Joseph found out about POPS through a friend. "I went to POPS to support my friend and ended up getting more involved than I expected. I am now vice president of POPS Venice, and my friend is president. I have met so many wonderful people and found myself in so many situations where I have had a positive impact on others. I will continue to be a loving person and be there for others."

J/U is a POPS club member.

King is the proud president of POPS the Club at James Monroe High School; he has been attending the club for two years and reminding everyone to remain resilient.

Kennedy King lives in Pennsylvania and is a member of the POPS club at Steelton Highspire. "I'm 16, I enjoy softball, art, cheerleading, and reading."

Reagan King lives in Pennsylvania and is a member of the POPS club at Steelton Highspire. She enjoys basketball, volleyball, BTS, and dancing. She played basketball and was a cheerleader.

KS is a member of POPS the Club at Venice High School in Los Angeles.

Eric Lee is a sophomore at Venice High School who finds joy in engaging in intellectual, historical, and political discussion.

Judith Lopez is a high school senior and a four-year member of POPS the Club. She is excited for the next chapter in her life, in which she hopes to pursue a career in the government and politics field.

Matthew Lopez is a senior at Culver City High School. He has lived in Highland Park, which is near East LA, and moved to Culver City when he began first grade and has lived there since.

Hiromi Maeda is a 17-year-old senior at Venice High. "I like to express my world and emotions through pictures. Photography is another way to share a story. For some, like myself, photography captures long-lasting memories that can always be something to look back on."

Alejandra Magallanes is a 2014 graduate of Venice High and a founding member of POPS the Club.

Nelvia Z. Marin-Caballero was a member of the first POPS club at Venice High, and her writings in this volume were first published in 2014 in the first POPS anthology, *Runaway Thoughts*. She loves POPS!

Ahidsa Mateo is a sophomore at Bronx Academy of Letters in New York City.

Leslie Mateos graduated from Venice High in 2015 and is a POPS the Club ambassador, speaker, and longtime member.

Kei'Arri Mcgruder is a forever member of POPS the Club, a graduate of Venice High School.

Nelson Mendez is an 18-year-old senior at Los Angeles High School of the Arts. He has been in POPS since freshman year and will miss the experience he got from it. He enjoys creating video content on YouTube, and you should check him out @nelsonm on YouTube :)

Jennifer Morrison has been an art educator for 20 years. She resides in Elizabethtown, PA, with her husband, son, and two Westies! She has been at the Steelton Highspire School District for 4 years and a POPS club advisor all 4 years. Jennifer was drawn to POPS because of her personal connection to the prison system. She knows about the pain that incarceration can bring to children and their families when a loved one becomes part of the costly, complex, and stressful prison environment.

Idalia Munoz graduated from Venice High School in 2014. She joined POPS her junior year and absolutely loved it. "I had the opportunity to meet so many people. We all came together one day out of the week to share these stories, truly incredible."

Brianna Carrington Myricks is a senior who believes coffee and murder mysteries are the best combination. Brianna is a helpful and caring daughter, a great friend, and a supportive sister. Her hobbies include listening to pop and dance music, watching teen TV shows, reading, and learning. She lives in LA with her family and two adorable dogs.

Alba Navas is a poet who strives to better understand others. She wrote her first poetry book at age 13 and has self-published two books. She is passionate about tennis, music, and photography and hopes to be a sports medicine physician.

Jaylynn "One Jay" Nelms is a POPS club member at Callaway Middle School in Georgia.

Janna Rae Nieto is 17 years old, a senior at Venice High, and a first-generation Filipo-American. "I have a passion for art in which I portray my everyday being and expression. I am constantly searching for inspiration, influence, and outlets to express myself. I want my work to manifest my ideas about life and possibly affect those who see it in a heartening way."

Luis Nunez was president of POPS the Club Venice High in 2014 and remains a forever supporter.

Guillermo Ovalle is a senior at the Bronx Academy of Letters in New York City.

Juliana Pinn is a student at Santa Monica High School, graduate of the class of 2020.

Stacie Ramirez is 16 years old and attends El Camino Real Charter High School. "I'm just trying to make it to senior year."

John Rodriguez is a POPS the Club board member and a recent graduate of UCLA. John was an early member of POPS the Club, and his writings in this volume were originally published in 2014 in the first POPS anthology, *Runaway Thoughts.*

Maricela Romero is a sophomore at Venice High School. "I live in Venice and have seen a lot."

Ellie Perez Sanchez is an outstanding and bright senior at LA High School of the Arts (LAHSA) who loves photography and science. She believes that anything can be achieved with authenticity, focus, effort, and time. "God has to be the first priority :)"

Giselle Sanchez is a POPS member and student at LA High School of the Arts.

Emanuel Scott is a member of the POPS club at Callaway Middle School in Georgia.

Katherine Secaida left LA to start over but realized she's not running anymore.

Imari Stevenson believes your past does not determine your future.

P.J. Swanson is a student in the POPS club at Culver High. "I try to be my best self, but sometimes my mentality gets in the way. Progress is being made; it's getting better."

Xavier Tucker is a POPS club member at Calloway Middle School.

Talena Vasquez is a member of POPS the Club at Venice High School.

Chris Wright is the philosopher-rockstar-surfer art teacher at Venice High and a longtime member of POPS the Club.

Tinsae Yimer is a member of the POPS club and a student at Venice High School.

Victor Zapata is a Venice High School POPS graduate whose interest in art developed into loving the duality of construction, from its design to its final build.

Acknowledgments

POPS stands for Pain of the Prison System, a name selected by the first cohort of students who gathered when the idea of providing a safe space for teens affected by incarceration was brand new. We launched in 2013 at Venice High School, and within weeks 25 students who had parents, siblings, or other loved ones in prison, jail, or detention—and a few who themselves had done time—began to gather. They knew at once the room was a safe space, a place where they discovered they were not alone and where they could tell their truths without being judged and feel the joy of a welcoming community. "POPS," they said, "yes, it stands for Pain of the Prison System, but POPS feels good the way the classroom feels when we're gathered together."

And there would be no POPS clubs, and thus no collection of artwork, poetry, and stories, without the principals who continue to welcome POPS into their schools or the school-based teacher-sponsors who dedicate their lunch or breakfast period each week to open their doors, hearts, and minds to host and co-lead these meetings. We are ever grateful to: Michael Alston, Nicole Bush, Ashlie Cotton, Kyle Denman, Gilda DeLaCruz, James DeLarme, Nicholas Griffen, Tina Gruen, Tuan Hophan, Michelle Lee, Reza Mir, Jose Montero, Robert Montes, Jennifer Morrison, Lizzy Mora, Zuri Placencia, Reggie Quemuel, Crissel Rodriguez, Sarah Rodriguez, Jesus Roman, Frederick Stanley, Shanika Sweeney, Stephanie Williams, Drake Witham, and Thomas Wu.

POPS clubs transform pain into hope and healing, and this year's anthology represents the work created by students in nearly every one of the 14 clubs across the country that have launched since our founding seven years ago. Today there are 8 clubs in Los Angeles, California (Culver City, El Camino Real Charter, James Monroe, LA High School of the Arts [LAHSA], Lawndale, New Village Girls Academy, and Santa Monica and Venice High Schools); 4 in Georgia (Callaway High School, Callaway Middle School, Carver High School, Long Cane Middle School); 1 in New York (Urban Assembly of Bronx Academy of Letters); and 1 in Pennsylvania (Steelton Highspire).

As teacher-sponsor Jennifer Morrison wrote in her introduction, we truly wish none of these young people needed a POPS Club, but we are grateful that for now there are a growing number of places where these resilient, wise young people are seen and heard.

We couldn't create these vital spaces and present our curriculum without the remarkable volunteers who devote their time, wisdom, leadership, and compassion to POPS youth. We wish to thank them: Devan Abhari, Phil America, Heather Bobula, Kristin Bungart, Hannah Kyle Crichton, Dennis Danziger, Sandy Danziger, Carmen De La Torre, Ann Devaney, Sonia Faye, Roberta (Riva) Goldman, Amy Gorton, Gigi Hooghkirk, Ann Kelly, Claire LaZebnik, Hannah Lewis, Latrice Lewis, Tracy Licenberg, Melissa Merritt, Judy Minor, Donald Murchie, Tricia Nelson, Vince Perata, Kate Savage, Laurie Sundell, Paul Surace, Roland Tec, and Casey Velasquez.

Without the generous guidance and support of our board of directors, our nonprofit would flounder. Thank you: Danny Alvarado, Dennis Danziger, Shalei Heflin, Austin Lindsey, Sonya Lowe, Hayley Macon, Nicole Misita, Oswaldo Navarro, Olivia Nelson, Aaron Palmer, John Rodriguez, Hannah Rogers, George Soneff, and Shandra Spicer.

Deepest gratitude to our wise advisors, critical and creative partners—too many to name them all, but special thanks to these: Pouyan Afkary, Robert Barton, Maureen Bernstein, Diane Botnick, Dana Buchman, Barbara Cendejas, Kelly Colbert, John Coleman, Dira Creek, Amber Cromwell, Bernardo Cubria, Sheldon Danziger, Rachel Davenport, Mike Davis, Karie DeLarme, Teri Ernst, David Faye, Marta Ferro, Rick Flatow, Myriam Forster, Vicky Foxworth, Sharon Goldinger, Ann Kelly, Kimberley Kyle, Andy Langdon, Susan Leonard, Fernando Lopez, Lauren Marks, Rose Martoma, Christina McDowell, Suzann Moskowitz, Julie Parrino, Patrick Record, Luis J. Rodriguez, Kate Savage, Suzanne Silverstein, Jessica Tuck, Jennifer Unger, Danielle Whylly, Boston Woodard, Jonathan Zeichner, and Kate Zentall.

Without funding, there would be no POPS at all. We are indebted to every one of our donors, to Guelaguetza Restaurante and Dinah's Family Restaurant for donating lunch each week to two of our schools, and gratitude abounding to our funders: The California Community Foundation, Liberty Hill Foundation and Los Angeles County Juvenile Probation Department's Ready to Rise Initiative; Hollywood Foreign Press Association; the Annenberg Foundation; the Audrey Irmas Foundation for Social Justice; the California Endowment; the California

Mental Health Services Authority; Carl & Roberta Deutsch Foundation; the Davis Family Foundation; the Gesner-Johnson Foundation; the Morris Hazan Family Foundation; the Judicate West Foundation; the Max Factor Family Foundation; Silicon Valley Community Foundation; Trial Lawyers' Charities LA; Wescom Credit Union We Care Foundation.

Words are insufficient to describe the dedication, passion, and heart of our staff. Thank you to our tireless interns, students, and graduates of the POPS program: Karen Arellano, Alexis Parish, Katherine Secaida, and Victor Zapata.

And to your boundless energy and creativity, thank you Valeria De La Torre, Sonia Faye, and Arielle Harris.

And to our longtime angel, Madge Stein Woods, our everlasting gratitude. You are always there, dear friend, with your boundless heart. Thank you.

Amy Friedman
Cofounder and Executive Director

I think as you're growing up, your emotions are just as deep as they are when you're an adult. Your ability to feel lonely, longing, confused, or angry are just as deep. We don't feel things more as we get older.

– *Spike Jonze*